The New Scriptwriter

The New Scriptwriter's Journal

by
Mary Charlotte Johnson

Focal Press
Taylor & Francis Group

NEW YORK AND LONDON

First published 2001

This edition published 2013
by Focal Press
70 Blanchard Road, Suite 402, Burlington, MA 01803

Simultaneously published in the UK
by Focal Press
2 Park Square, Milton Park, Abingdon, Oxon OX14 4RN

Focal Press is an imprint of the Taylor & Francis Group, an informa business

Notices

Practitioners and researchers must always rely on their own experience and knowledge in evaluating and using any information, methods, compounds, or experiments described herein. In using such information or methods they should be mindful of their own safety and the safety of others, including parties for whom they have a professional responsibility.

To the fullest extent of the law, neither the Publisher nor the authors, contributors, or editors, assume any liability for any injury and/or damage to persons or property as a matter of products liability, negligence or otherwise, or from any use or operation of any methods, products, instructions, or ideas contained in the material herein.

Library of Congress Cataloging-in-Publication Data

Johnson, Mary Charlotte.
   The new scriptwriter's journal/by Mary Charlotte Johnson. —2nd ed.
      p.   cm.
   Rev. ed. of: Scriptwriter's journal. © 1995.
   Includes bibliographical references and index.
   ISBN 13: 978-0-240-80384-5 (pbk)
   1. Motion picture authorship.   2. Television authorship.   I. Johnson, Mary Charlotte. Scriptwriter's journal.   II. Title.
PN1996.J63   2001
808.2′3—dc21   00-41743

British Library Cataloguing-in-Publication Data
A catalogue record for this book is available from the British Library.

For Veronica and Jacqueline
Too dear for this earth

Contents

Preface

As I embarked on the journey of revising this edition, I realized how much has changed since the first edition. This edition is not just an update; it's an open-ended exploration of what the future might hold for aspiring scriptwriters.

This may be the single most exciting time for scriptwriters to be exploring the field. With the advent of digital technology, the face of filmmaking is changing forever. What this means for you, the scriptwriter, is that you will have a more active role in scripting your own life. Right now, not in some distant future, you're capable of scripting, shooting and editing your own work with a digital camera and desktop computer. As technology becomes more sophisticated, the process will be democratized to an even greater extent.

Does this mean you should abandon the craft? Certainly not. In fact, since there may be fewer systems filtering material in the future, it's more relevant than ever that you learn the craft of scriptwriting. Problems should always be solved at the script stage. Fixing a work in post is not a desirable option. No matter which medium you use to tell a story, you need to learn to solve problems and formulate questions. As new technologies arrive, new questions, often complex questions, arise.

It will be your task to lead the thinking, push the limits, and help us remember what's vital to us as humans. The storytelling of the future resides in you.

Today's scriptwriting is a new enterprise, even for seasoned scriptwriters. Options are limitless. Boundaries are breaking down. Traditional script structures are being challenged. You may be writing for film, television, the Internet, games, virtual reality, or story worlds we've not yet imagined. Your future as a scriptwriter, as well as your journey, may well begin between these pages . . .

Acknowledgments

Once again, everyone at Focal Press has been terrific—and very patient. Special thanks to Terri Jadick for her positive feedback, to Jennifer Plumley for her guidance, and to Marie Lee for her continued support.

My sincere appreciation to Steven Schutzman for permission to reprint his story, "The Bank Robbery." Thanks, too, to Diane Dutra, Bret Kane, and Michael Ozias for sharing their journal entries.

This edition would not have been possible without the tireless research efforts of Jaime Carol George, who provided extensive help updating the text and invaluable suggestions for additions. She also wrote a beautiful foreword not included in this text but retained soundly and fondly in memory. Thanks, too, to Chris Van Cleef for his additional help with current film industry statistics, his steady support of my writing efforts, and his abiding friendship.

Shamefully, in the first edition, I neglected to mention a few people who've helped make my journey richer. Thanks and grins to Leslie Jordan and Lynn Anderson for being true sisters and vital life forces; Dorothy and Glenn Hershberger for embracing my daughter, Leah, and I when we were adrift; Maria Methven, for teaching me the true meaning of courage, tenacity and humor; Deb Berry for the goddess that she is; and the Haxan guys for including me as part of their extended family and reviving my faith (sometimes good guys do finish first). No doubt I've forgotten others. If you count yourselves among them, thanks in advance for forgiving me my flaws and loving me.

Lastly, thanks to Jim Gunshanan for remaining a constant surprise and for his love.

PART I
The Creative Process

The Inner Journey

There is an internal landscape, a geography of the soul; we search for its outlines all our lives.[1]

—Josephine Hart

This is the scene. You're in a crowded, noisy bookstore leafing through these pages. Or you're in your home by the fireplace snuggling up to read this book. Undoubtedly, you're asking yourself, "Why is every other page blank?" Good question.

The blank pages are designed to induce, provoke, tease, and challenge you to write. These journal pages provide space for scribbling, sketching, observing, recording, sensing, rambling, musing, gossiping, and dreaming. Jot down daydreams, night dreams, nightmares, fears, fantasies, memories—anything that moves you.

In a very real sense, you and I will share authorship of this book. By the time you've finished reading and writing, you'll not only have the knowledge to tackle writing a script, you'll also have a personal journal that will serve as a sourcebook of ideas for your scripts.

What's that you're thinking? Journals are a nuisance. You had to keep a journal in the fifth grade and you hated it. Besides, you don't have time. There's work, grad school, dishes, kids, the lawn needs to be mowed, the car needs a new carburetor, the dog needs a flea bath, the bills need to be paid.

Relax. No excuses are necessary. No one is going to check to see if you're writing in your journal. You won't be graded on its contents. You won't lose your job if you don't write in it. No one else needs to read your journal if you choose to write in it.

A journal is for you and you only. All of our lives we've been conditioned to produce for others—parents, teachers, clergy, bosses,

colleagues, spouses, in-laws, children, friends, lovers. Our pleasure is often derived from pleasing others. Certainly pleasing others is a worthwhile goal, but sometimes it distracts us from our own needs. Sometimes it distracts us from ourselves.

Your journal is an open invitation to rediscover yourself. Consider it a gift to yourself. The pages of your journal offer a place to be alone, to indulge your fantasies, to confess your fears, to discover secrets you've kept from yourself, to explore worlds within worlds.

If you're reluctant to begin writing, don't worry. This book is designed to encourage you. Periodically, you'll be provided with specific writing prompts to stimulate your thinking and help you begin the process of writing. If you don't need the prompts, ignore them. Remember, this is *your* journal.

Each writing prompt is designed to complement ideas as they are presented within the reading. Responding to writing prompts is a form of freewriting, or what Henriette Klauser calls "rapidwriting." Rapidwriting is an uninhibited, fluid form of writing that lets "the words spill out without stopping to critique or correct or rearrange." In her book *Writing on Both Sides of the Brain*, Klauser maintains that because the right and left hemispheres of the brain perform different functions, writers experience an inherent conflict. The right side of the brain wants to ramble and explore, while the left side of the brain wants to dominate and edit, even as a writer is thinking.[2]

Klauser suggests that writers reconcile the hemispheres of the brain by learning to separate the act of writing from the act of editing during rapidwriting. You may find this a difficult challenge. If you're one of those writers who constantly edits while you write, you'll have to make a conscious effort to separate writing from editing.

If you're a compulsive editor, you'll probably appreciate this story from the book *Walking on Alligators*. As the author, Susan Shaughnessy, tells it:

> A friend of mine used to joke that if she left a manuscript out on the desk at night, she feared the cleaning crew would not be able to resist the temptation to edit it. Then it really happened to her.
>
> She came in to work and found some notes attached to a manuscript. In neat handwriting, the writer explained that she was an English student at a nearby university. She cleaned office buildings at night to work her way through school. She had become interested in the manuscript, left out in the center of the tidy desk, and wanted to make some suggestions.[3]

Rapidwriting discourages the editor in you and encourages the writer in you. Though it may take extra effort at first, try rapidwriting when you respond to the prompts. The only rule is to write with abandon.

Don't worry about spelling or sloppiness or sentences—just write as fast as you can. Eventually, you'll rapidwrite without thinking, and you may be surprised at what bubbles to the surface while you're writing.

This first prompt should provoke you to think about yourself as a writer. When responding to prompts, always write honest responses and the first answers that come to mind. Don't try to intellectualize. Write from your gut.

Rapidwrite a short story in which a writer attempts to murder his or her editor. What is the writer's motivation for murder? Is the writer successful? If not, does the editor seek revenge? Be playful. Take chances. Be absurd. Think of all the soap opera characters who've been killed only to return again under mysterious circumstances. Loosen up those cerebral muscles and stretch.

Now, describe the process you undertook while writing. Was it hard to write a story? Describe yourself as a writer. Do you enjoy writing? If not, why not? Is there anything that you'd change about yourself as a writer if you could? Think about the way in which you write. Do you write with little restraint, rereading and cleaning up the text from time to time? If so, you're probably a latent editor as well as a writer. Do you frequently stop, reread what you've written, and go back and rewrite as you're writing? Do you have trouble getting on with your writing because you get stuck editing instead? If so, you're probably a compulsive editor. Maybe you write without much care and see editing as an irritating task. Maybe you're a rapidwriter all the time. If so, do you feel satisfied that your writing is in its most polished form when you've finished?

Asking you questions is a way for me to engage you in written dialogue. A form of "talking" to me through your writing, written dialogue is a kind of conversation between writers. In an ideal setting, we would write back and forth to one another. For our purposes here, I'll share thoughts and open-ended questions that invite you to "converse" with me. If something you read evokes an emotion, "speak" to me about what you're feeling. If something I suggest seems preposterous, "argue" with me. You'll always win the argument because I won't be able to "talk" back.

Written dialogue is a natural extension of what Lev Vygotsky calls inner speech, a form of "talking" to yourself manifest in verbal thought. In his book *Thought and Language*, Vygotsky maintains that, at an early age, language begins as a dialogue with the self.[4] Think about your "self" as a child. Did you talk to your "self" or to imaginary playmates? Maybe those imaginary playmates that you conversed with helped you make meaning of the

world. As a child, you may have had the solitude during playtime to listen to your inner speech. Oftentimes as an adult, your responsibilities may distract you enough that you forget to listen to your inner speech.

Writing creates a unique opportunity for you to listen to your inner speech, to reacquaint you with your self, for it is through the process of composing thoughts that the self becomes fully realized. Since writing is a metacognitive act, you necessarily think about thinking as you compose; that is, you try to understand and reflect upon your own thought processes. As the poet John Ashbery reflects, "I write to find out what I'm thinking."[5] Writing forces thought forth. During the process of writing, your inner speech resounds through your written words, taking you on the first step to the interior landscape of the self.

This landscape, this inner world, is where the self resides. Have you been to this inner world? Do you know how to find it? Can you imagine it? In *Writing for Your Life,* Deena Metzger describes this mysterious territory. See if you recognize the place.

> It is the world of worlds. It is infinite. To enter it is to come to know something of it and to learn of the boundlessness of the self. To go within, therefore, is never diminishment. To stay adamantly without is always a limitation, for the self, the inner world, the imagination, all open out into everything that has ever existed or can ever or may exist. . . . Like any unexplored territory, it will, each time, turn out to be both strange and familiar. And we go into it, each time, as if we have never been there before and also as if we are coming home.[6]

THE JOURNEY

For you, the scriptwriter, your task is not to discover what formula will create the best product; your task is to forage through the interior landscape of the self to discover a story worth telling. As you search for that story, you may discover a quiet truth—the journey is where the self is actualized.

The center of this actualization resides within your imagination. What is the imagination? Kris Kringle, portrayed by Edmund Gwenn, answers that question in the original version of the film *Miracle on 34th Street.*

> To me, the imagination is a place all by itself. A separate country. Now, you've heard of the French nation, the British nation—well, this is the imagination. It's a wonderful place. How would you like to be able to make snowballs in the summertime, eh? Or drive a great big bus right down Fifth Avenue? How would you like to have a ship all to yourself that makes daily trips to China? Australia? How would you like to be the Statue of Liberty in the morning and in the afternoon fly south with a flock of

geese? Very simple. But it takes practice. Now, the first thing you've got to learn is how to pretend.[7]

As adults we sometimes find it difficult to remember how to pretend, yet imaginative thinking is vital to the discovery of the self. In *The Lone Ranger and Tonto Fistfight in Heaven*, fiction writer, poet, and screenwriter Sherman Alexie (*Smoke Signals, Indian Killer*) articulates how necessary the imagination is to both the discovery as well as the sustenance of the self.

> Imagination is the politics of dreams; imagination turns every word into a bottle rocket . . . Imagine an escape. Imagine that your own shadow on the wall is a perfect door. Imagine a song stronger than penicillin. Imagine a drum which wraps itself around your heart. Imagine a story that puts wood in the fireplace.[8]

Now stop reading for a moment and try writing again. Borrowing from Alexie's passage, "imagine that your own shadow on the wall is a perfect door." Try walking through that door. Where does it take you? Describe the world you imagine. Who do you encounter in this world? Do you want to remain in this world or return to the world from which you came? Is it easy for you to imagine other worlds? Do you often fantasize or daydream?

Fantasies and daydreams represent far more than capricious longings. By projecting yourself into other worlds, you're shaping who you're becoming. Imagination becomes a significant contributor to the constantly shifting essence of your existence. As Edward Murray, author of *Imaginative Thinking and Human Existence*, elaborates:

> Seen from this perspective the imagination moves from the periphery of existence to the center of actuality. It is human thought now setting the stage for the creation of actuality, for the birth of being, for the realization of possibilities, for the construction of life and transformation of one's existence.[9]

If you accept this view, writing is not only a way of knowing, it is a way of becoming a fully realized human being.

In order to consciously move toward becoming, you must be able to enter the imaginative realm. This task requires energy, intellect, hope, tenacity, and great courage, since the terrain is often terrifying. There are no road maps, no road signs, no familiar markers to ease you along the path. You must enter at your own risk.

The risk involves facing truths about yourself that you may wish to avoid. Once you've entered, you may not be able to turn back. In Eleanor Coppola's documentary, *Hearts of Darkness: A Filmmaker's Apocalypse*, she describes the journey that her then-husband Francis experienced as he directed and wrote (co-authored with John Milius) *Apocalypse Now*, based on the novel by Joseph Conrad.

> The film Francis is making is a metaphor for a journey into self. He has made that journey and is still making it. It's scary to watch someone you love go into the center of himself and confront his fears—fear of failure, fear of death, fear of going insane. You have to fail a little, die a little, go insane a little, to come out the other side.[10]

Even an artist of Francis Ford Coppola's esteem experiences grave doubts during the journey inward.

Self-doubt can paralyze you. It's natural to be afraid of failure—no one wants to fail. But unless you're willing to plunge deep into the center of yourself, you will never have the satisfaction of having faced your fears and gone beyond them.

Can you avoid facing those truths and still tell a good story? Perhaps, but you'll be cheating yourself. The value of the inner journey lies in the experience. For whether the story is ultimately a success or a failure, the experience is invaluable. Time is never wasted on a journey well traveled, never wasted on becoming.

To become you must enter the imaginative realm. To enter that world you must pass through chaos. In order to claim our imaginative powers, Ann E. Berthoff suggests in *The Making of Meaning* that we order chaos.[11] This ordering of chaos is a complex, highly individualistic process. In subsequent chapters you'll learn strategies that will help you find a path through the labyrinth that is the mind. There are no formulaic methods for ordering chaos, no equations for shaping stories. You must find your own way through the interior landscape of the self. Sometimes it's a journey of utter joy, sometimes a journey of dark confusion. Always it's a journey of necessity.

How would you describe your "self"? If you could script your life, what journey would you imagine for yourself? If you were in the editing room watching a film about your life, what would you edit? What fragments of film would find their way to the cutting room floor? What new scenes would you shoot for the sequel?

REFERENCES

1. Josephine Hart, *Damage*, Ivy Books, New York, 1991, p. 1.
2. Henriette Anne Klauser, *Writing on Both Sides of the Brain: Breakthrough Techniques for People Who Write*, Harper, San Francisco, 1987, p. 15.
3. Susan Shaughnessy, *Walking on Alligators: A Book of Meditations for Writers*, Harper, San Francisco, 1993, p. 16.
4. Lev S. Vygotsky, *Thought and Language*, trans. Eugenia Hanfmann and Gertrude Vakar, The M.I.T. Press, Cambridge, 1962, p. 22.
5. Joshua Cooper Ramo and Debra Rosenberg, "The Puzzle of Genius," *Newsweek*, June 28, 1993, p. 50. Original source not given.
6. Deena Metzger, *Writing for Your Life: A Guide and Companion to the Inner Worlds*, Harper, San Francisco, 1992, p. 7.
7. George Seaton, *Miracle on 34th Street* (based on an original story by Valentine Davis), 20th Century Fox, 1947.
8. Sherman Alexie, *The Lone Ranger and Tonto Fistfight in Heaven*, Harper Perennial, New York, 1994, pp. 152–153.
9. Edward L. Murray, *Imaginative Thinking and Human Existence*, Duquesne University Press, Pittsburgh, Pennsylvania, 1986, p. 62.
10. Eleanor Coppola, *Hearts of Darkness: A Filmmaker's Apocalypse*, ZM Productions, 1991.
11. Ann E. Berthoff, *The Making of Meaning*, Boynton, Upper Montclair, New Jersey, 1981, p. 77.

2

The Writing Process

*I'm not sure I understand the process of writing. There is, I'm sure,
something strange about imaginative concentration. The brain slowly begins
to function in a different way, to make mysterious connections.*[1]

—Elizabeth Hardwick

When you sit down to write, keep in mind that writing is not a formulaic act that culminates in a product. Writing is a process that takes you
on an inner journey from which you must make order out of chaos, from
which you must find what Coleridge called the "shaping spirit of imagination," from which you must discover a story worth telling.

The writing process proceeds in proximate phases. Just as creating a
film involves preproduction, production, and postproduction, writing
shares a parallel process that, in simplest terms, can be reduced to pre-
writing, writing, and postwriting. **Conceptualizing**, **actualizing**, and
redacting more precisely describe the phases of the process. Yet it would
be fallacious to believe that the phases are clearly delineated. Movement
among phases occurs as stories take shape. The purpose of identifying
phases is to clarify what occurs while you're writing.

CONCEPTUALIZING

Before you actualize your ideas in writing, you abstract them internally.
This constitutes the conceptualizing phase of the writing process. Because
this phase of the process can't be observed externally, it's a difficult stage
to define. Perhaps Victor Hugo said it best when he observed, "A man is
not idle because he is absorbed in thought. There is a visible labor and there
is an invisible labor."[2] Conceptualizing is invisible labor.

17

The term conceptualizing is derived from the Latin word *concipire*, meaning "to take to oneself." This internal taking to oneself is a time of germination when the seeds of ideas grow. Like dandelion seeds, they may drift in from a distant wind; like watermelon seeds, they may be fired dead center; like maple seeds, they may flutter to the ground and burrow deep into the damp soil.

The seeds of thought find fertile ground in the open intellect that recognizes the value of intuitive as well as rational knowledge. Jacques Maritain, author of *Creative Intuition in Art and Poetry*, refers to intuitive knowledge as magical knowledge.

> An obscure knowledge through inclination—born in the preconscious of the spirit—in which the world is known *in* and *through* the subjectivity, grasped both together and inseparably by means of an emotion become intentional and intuitive. Such a knowledge is utterly different from what we ordinarily call knowledge, it is more experience than knowledge.[3]

Intuitive knowledge emerges in and through the emotions, the senses, the spirit, the inner reserves of the imagination. This knowledge often slips into the conscious mind in fragments—bits of words, memories, melodies, fragrances, images. These fragments become a shorthand from the preconscious, nudging the conscious mind into action. As Frank Capra quipped, "A hunch is creativity trying to tell you something."[4]

Tug at your creativity as you try responding to the next prompt. Remember, an open intellect invites expression through intuitive knowledge.

Write from the point of view of a seed. What kind of seed are you? Describe your view, your destination, what you're thinking or feeling—anything that might assist you in discovering a seed's point of view.

When I ask writers to respond to the seed prompt, I'm amazed by the range and ingenuity of their responses. One of my former students, Bret Kane, wrote a journal entry that remains one of my favorites.

> Boy, I sure am glad to be working for John. I mean, gee whiz how many of us actually get to work for the famous Mr. A.? There is so much work to be done though, at dawn we start the attack and hopefully we'll be able to capture this whole field and hill. It's gonna be tough though and we gotta work fast. Once we're underway we hafta spread out fast and find cover. "The real battle is won and lost in the trenches boys!" That's what Mr. A told us. We're a team though and we'll dig in hard and fast when you work for a man like John, you feel inspired. I mean ho seeds actually get to work for Johnny Appleseed?

Bret applied his intuitive knowledge of the proud feelings of a naive foot soldier to his rational knowledge of planting, history, and myth. Though Bret's entry illustrates the symbiotic relationship between intuitive and rational knowledge, it's important to remember that expression is rooted in intuitive knowledge.

How do you tap into your intuitive knowledge? You might try beginning with your senses. Just as you might imagine a basket of fruit on your kitchen table, try imagining a basket of sensations. What's in the basket? Maybe the soft rhythm of a baby breathing; a single drop of dew silently sliding down a glossy leaf; gardenias browning at the edges, their heady fragrance thinning to nothingness; stains from rotting cherries bloodying sun-blanched city sidewalks; snow melting instantly on a hot tongue; a cat's rough tongue licking an empty bowl; the animal smell of human skin darkening in the midday sun; a child patting wet sand into turrets and tunnels fed by a channel of salt water from the pounding sea.

You might also tap into your intuitive knowledge through memories. Dig out some old records or tapes and listen to the music in the dark. What do you see? What do you remember? Does it take you back to another place and time? Does it evoke memories of someone who has had a powerful influence in your life? Think of those persons who have influenced you significantly. Who has influenced you most positively? Who has had the most negative influence?

As you attempt to shape thoughts into forms, to order chaos, you may find that your thought process spins in a spiral rather than a linear fashion. Your mind dreams, stretches, visualizes, hesitates, dreams, stretches, visualizes, hesitates, hesitates, hesitates. Though hesitation may be an indication of your fear of beginning to write, it also may be a sign of inner turmoil. You need to be truthful enough with yourself to distinguish between hesitation as sign and hesitation as fear.

Hesitation as sign may be your inner speech warning you that the territory is dangerous. You may have an idea that plays in your mind like a melody that you can't identify, that lingers, haunts you, triggers the vague outline of a distant memory. Write through your hesitation in your journal. By describing your frustration, you may unveil the source of your hesitation.

Here's a writing prompt that may help you unlock the secrets you keep from yourself. Imagine this:

You awake in strange surroundings. You have no memory of who you are or where you are. Is this your home? You begin to investigate the surroundings, rummage through the belongings of the person who lives here. Maybe you question a neighbor. What do you learn about this stranger, yourself?

If you still aren't close to shaping your idea into a workable form, put that idea aside and work on another. Your hesitation may mean you're not ready to explore that territory because it's too painful or too truthful for you to handle at the present time. Don't worry—if the idea is important, it will resurface later. Sometimes an idea will lie dormant like a volcano, then erupt as a fiery surprise when you least expect it.

Hesitation as fear is a natural occurrence that almost all writers encounter. What are your fears when you sit down to write? Are you afraid that your story is terrible, that your work is mediocre at best, that you're a failure at life as well as at writing, that everyone will now know that you're an imposter who can't write, or that ruthless critics will destroy your career? You're not alone. All writers face similar fears.

I often become quite obsessive when I hesitate out of fear. My backyard usually looks wild enough to qualify as a nature preserve. Yet when I'm faced with writing, I'll find the means to mow, trim, and fertilize under Florida's scorching sun. Most writers will confess similar avoidance tactics. Fran Lebowitz admits, "When I'm supposed to be writing I clean my apartment, take my clothes to the laundry, get organized, make lists, do the dishes. I would never do a dish unless I had to write."[5]

Ironically, doing the dishes may be the best time to conceptualize. Because the task requires little attention, the mind is free to play with ideas. In fact, vital conceptual thought often occurs in the most mundane moments. Maybe you're alone, sipping coffee at a fast-food restaurant at two in the morning. The smell of the coffee evokes a memory. You scribble ideas on a coffee-stained napkin. Those ideas become the germinal seeds for your next script.

Sometimes the ideas shoot through your brain faster than you can write them down. Alfred Hitchcock was such an active conceptual thinker that he visualized whole films, shot-by-shot, in his mind. That's why he found writing scripts tedious; since he had already "seen" the film, scriptwriting was reduced to transcribing.

Sometimes ideas tumble around in your mind for years. William Goldman wrote *Butch Cassidy and the Sundance Kid* in four weeks but it took him eight years to research and conceptualize the story. It doesn't matter whether it takes years or weeks or days or minutes or seconds to conceptualize a story. In the world of abstract thought, time is not measured in finite terms.

Write about time. Is time important to you? Do you use your time well? How often do you think about time? Do you spend more time thinking about what you ought to be doing than it would actually take to complete the task? Do you worry about not having enough time? Have you ever

had an experience in which you wanted to manipulate time; that is, you wanted to make the experience last much longer or you wanted the experience to end quickly? Describe that experience.

Diana Hunt and Pam Hait, the authors of *The Tao of Time*, offer significant insight regarding time. "Understand that there is no destination in time. The journey is the process."[6] Having no destination frees writers to live most intensely in the moment, to immerse themselves in the immediacy of the present, to live in and through experience, to notice.

Observation is a necessity. As a writer, you need to notice everything. No detail is too small, no moment insignificant. As a writer, you need to discover the extraordinary in the ordinary. When paired with the imagination, observation provokes new thought, creates poetic vision. Consider this example from Alan Lightman's novel *Einstein's Dreams*, a fictive imagining of how Einstein conceptualized the theory of relativity through observation.

> A mushy, brown peach is lifted from the garbage and placed on the table to pinken. It pinkens, it turns hard, it is carried in a shopping sack to the grocer's, put on a shelf, removed and crated, returned to the tree with pink blossoms. In this world, time flows backward.[7]

Pairing observation with imagination signifies the stirrings of metaphorical thought.

To think metaphorically, you must make connections among the disparate visions, remembrances, and observations that crowd your mind. This requires that you break down categories, strip away the familiar, disassemble logical connections, and imagine that which was previously unimaginable.

Metaphorical thought leads to the gradual ordering of chaos. As you seek to make metaphorical connections, you begin to reinvent your thinking, to grasp for imaginative fusion between the things of the world and the moments of your life. By juxtaposing seemingly dissimilar concepts, your mind explores the complexities of tension, paradox, polarization, contradiction, and ambiguity. In this enigmatic process, you integrate what might at first appear to be incongruous parts into a meaningful whole.

Think of your mind as a kaleidoscope. Each of your ideas is a colorful fragment of a whole integrated in a design that catches the light. As you turn the kaleidoscope, the colors realign, creating new shapes and reflections. When you write, you need to keep turning your ideas and realigning your thoughts until the light you capture creates a startling vision.

Once you have this vision, your ideas will fall into place. As the shape of your story emerges, concepts become characters. As your story grows,

you begin to move toward the next phase of the writing process—actualizing. In this phase, you act on your ideas.

ACTUALIZING

During the actualizing phase of the writing process, your ideas are realized in action. When a scene in a film is ready to be shot, the director yells "Action!" The action really begins long before the cameras roll. The action begins when you begin to act.

To act for a writer means to write. Sounds like an understatement, doesn't it? Yet countless people claim to be writers who have yet to pick up a pen, peck away at a typewriter, or click the keys of a computer. Imagining that you're a writer doesn't make you a writer. Having an idea doesn't make you a writer. Pitching a concept doesn't make you a writer. Writing makes you a writer.

Writing has been romanticized as a mythical process that magically happens to the receptive artist. Though magical connections may occur when you write, writing is not a magical process. Writing is wrestling with words until you sweat.

There are no detours around writing. You have to grit your teeth and plow straight ahead. Writing requires dedication and discipline. In order to write, you must commit your ideas to the page. Even if you believe you're committed, you won't accomplish much if you don't discipline yourself to write on a regular basis.

Having the discipline to write requires that you be your own boss. Being your own boss has definite advantages—you create your own hours and working conditions; the only person you have to answer to is yourself. But to be effective, you must be self-reliant. If you don't write on a regular basis, if you don't meet your self-imposed deadlines, you'll never finish your story. Thus, to succeed as a writer, you must be a diligent boss.

Your diligence as a boss depends upon your ability to establish time-lines for yourself. Every week, you should establish goals. This may mean that you set up a daily or weekly quota for yourself, measured in time or pages or both. You might say to yourself, "I'm going to write for one hour every day this week," or "I'm going to write five pages a day every day this week." At the end of the week, assess your success. Were you able to meet your goals? If you were, reward yourself. In fact, it's a good idea to build in a reward. Promise yourself that if you accomplish your goal you'll do something special for yourself: spend a night with a friend, read a book, go to a concert or the beach or a film—whatever works for you.

If you weren't able to reach your goals, why not? Sometimes you have legitimate reasons; more often you have few reasons but plenty of excuses, excuses, excuses. Excuses prohibit you from writing. Think of all the

energy it takes to create elaborate excuses for yourself. Why not apply some of that imaginative energy to the creation of a good story?

Just as a mason constructs a building brick by brick, a writer builds a story word by word. Part of your task as a writer is to stack up the words. The secret to becoming a fine writer is to keep writing. Write and write and write without worrying about whether the words are brilliant. You can always write another draft. As screenwriter Anna Hamilton Phelan (*In Love and War*, *Mask*, *Into the Homeland*, *Gorillas in the Mist*, *Girl Interrupted*, and *Chains*) advises, "Don't worry about what's going to happen to this. Just write the next word."[8]

Let your story unfold. It's important to get the words out as fast as you're able so you don't lose the story's inspiration and passion. Even if the structure is not yet in place, or the characters are not fully realized, it's vital that you push forward. There is an energy, an impetus present in the early stages of a work that may be lost if you don't capture the initial impulse.

There will be times when you're writing that you have the urge to go back, to rewrite, to reformulate your ideas. This is an expected part of the actualizing phase. Writing is recursive in nature; that is, you move backward as well as forward when you're writing. This backward-moving action compels you to go back to the text you've already written before you can go forward. "In other words, recursiveness in writing implies that there is a forward-moving action that exists by virtue of a backward-moving action."[9]

You may reread what you've already written and decide that a description, a character, a scene, or the direction of the storyline needs to be rewritten. Once you've reached this conclusion, you need to decide whether you should rewrite now or later. If you have to reconceptualize an element of your story, you may want to solve the perceived problem before writing any further. If the problem is superficial or you can write around the problem, keep writing. There's danger in rewriting so extensively that you can't move forward.

Make sure you create realistic expectations for yourself. Don't expect perfection. You're creating a first draft that should be treated as such. The first draft of your script is a malleable shape awaiting refinement. That refinement occurs in the redacting phase of the writing process.

Think about the word "act." What does it mean to you? Think about your past actions. Do you regret any of those actions? Did you ever "act up" in school? If so, what did you do and what was the outcome? Did you ever act in a play? If so, what was the play and what part did you play? How did you feel inside the skin of a character? Even if you've never been

in a play, you may find yourself acting. Do your actions change when you are with different people in different places? Think about how you act when you're with your family, your friends, your enemies. Do you act differently when you're at work, at the mall, in school, in church, or in the car with your lover? If so, why? What if you went to a new place where you knew no one? How would you act?

REDACTING

Simply stated, redacting is editing—the revising process that makes a work suitable for publication or presentation. Derived from the Latin word *redact*, its literal meaning is "to drive back." For you, the scriptwriter, this driving back thrusts you back to your first draft.

As an observant writer, you've probably noticed that the word "acting" is embedded in the word redacting. This is no accident. When you redact, you act again. For the scriptwriter, to act again is to rewrite.

Redacting is not just about rewriting, however. To redact is to reflect, refine, and in some cases, to reconceptualize. To redact is to frame questions about your original work.

In order to frame questions, imagine yourself as someone else in a dark theatre watching your story on the screen for the first time. Does the story immediately capture your attention? Can you follow the storyline? Is there a consistent logic in the world you've created? Does the story sustain your interest? Does the story have surprises? Is the ending predictable or provocative? Does the story ask you to consider ideas about which you've never thought?

These questions are intended to help you focus on what is needed for the rewrite. Keep in mind that these particular questions may not be suitable for your story. Are these the questions you should be asking yourself or should you be posing other questions? Are you capable of answering questions about your own story objectively?

Objectivity is difficult, if not impossible, to attain. After working for weeks, months, or years on a script, you may be unable to divorce your intellect from the passion you feel for your work. You're too close to the script. This is compounded by the fact that you may have limited experience formulating questions about your own work.

Scriptwriting is a unique writing profession since there is no formal editing process. No professional editor makes substantive comments. No copy editor corrects syntactical errors. No one nurtures you. No one protects you. Just as you must be your own boss, you must also be your own editor.

To be your own editor, you must learn to ask yourself the right questions, trust your own judgment, make informed choices, and seek

suggestions from others whom you respect. As your own editor, you need to nurture your style. You must also identify weaknesses in individual scenes or in the script as a whole and devise strategies for strengthening the script. Additionally, you must make sure the final draft of the script looks professional, free from grammatical and typographical errors.

How do you decide where the script needs work? Listen carefully to your inner speech and you'll hear a persistent voice nagging. At first, you may only sense there is a problem. Listen again. Reread the script or portions of the story that you feel aren't working. This takes practice and the ability to be truthful with yourself, but eventually you'll be able to target specific problems.

Usually you'll already know there are problems before you finish the first draft. It's a good idea to note troublesome places in the story as you're writing. By identifying specific areas of concentration while you're writing, you'll find the process of rewriting easier.

How many drafts of a script should you write? Only you can answer that question. You'll know when you get there. It's not unusual for professional scriptwriters to write four or more drafts of a script before they're satisfied. Screenwriters Joel and Ethan Coen offer their advice.

> How much is too much? When do you quit?
> Even did he wish to, the critic couldn't answer, for he doesn't know. He might believe that you quit revising a manuscript when it is "right." He might also believe that a bell sounds on the floor of the stock exchange when the Dow has reached its high for the day. Neither will the professional writer tell you the rule for when to stop writing, because he is insecure, fearful of giving up trade secrets and losing his competitive edge. *We'll* tell you, because we're in the movie business and so our careers depend upon public caprice rather than on the play of competitive market forces. The rule is, you quit rewriting when your manuscript starts to bore you. Only the amateur, who has boundless energy and who lacks the imagination to quit, ever works beyond that point.
> Consult, then, your heart. Once your work feels stale and tiresome you should present it to the public. Anyway, that's what we do.[10]

Just be sure you've told a great story, presented in a professional format, penned in a highly readable style. If you have, your script will become what's referred to as a **calling card script**—the script that best represents you as a writer.

One of the greatest mistakes you can make is to circulate your script before it's ready. Always reveal your strengths as a writer by showing off your best work. Keep in mind that your best work may not emerge until you've written many drafts of many scripts. With each script you write, you'll learn more about yourself and the craft of scriptwriting, and you'll

gain the confidence necessary to write the script that will bring you deserved recognition.

Don't be discouraged. Think of what a rare privilege it is to travel the road to your inner life. What other endeavor permits you to create new worlds and populate those worlds with any beings you might imagine? Where else can you go to be totally free to explore your feelings, your fears, and your fantasies? If you kindle your imagination, your writing will burn with energy.

This energy is necessary to fuel the writing process. As you now know, writing is an active process. Movement among the phases is a natural outcome of the process. As you're actualizing, you may find it necessary to return to the conceptualizing phase of the process. As you're redacting, it may be necessary to return to the actualizing phase of the process.

Understanding the process doesn't always help you solve the problems that occur as you write, however. To solve writing problems, you need to have strategies for creative problem solving. The next chapter will provide you with practical skills to help you identify problems and solve them creatively.

Think about "driving back." What thoughts would you like to "drive back" from your mind? Now drive back in your memory to when you first drove a car. Can you remember what you felt, what being behind the wheel represented for you? Do you still feel the same way about driving? If you could drive the car in the movie *Back to the Future*, to what time period would you travel? Who would you take with you, if anyone?

REFERENCES

1. Amber Coverdale Sumrall, ed., *Write to the Heart: Wit and Wisdom of Women Writers*, The Crossing Press, Freedom, California, 1992, p. 39. Original source not cited.
2. John-Roger and Peter McWilliams, *The Portable Life 101*, Prelude Press, Los Angeles, 1992, p. 119. Original source not cited.
3. Jacques Maritain, *Creative Intuition in Art and Poetry*, Princeton University Press, Princeton, New Jersey, 1953, pp. 184–185.
4. Susan Shaughnessy, *Walking on Alligators: A Book of Meditations for Writers*, Harper, San Francisco, 1993, p. 39. Original source not cited.
5. Henriette Anne Klauser, *Writing on Both Sides of the Brain: Breakthrough Techniques for People Who Write*, Harper, San Francisco, 1987, p. 56. Original source not cited.
6. Diana Hunt, Ph.D., and Pam Hait, *The Tao of Time*, Henry Holt and Company, New York, 1990, p. 63.

7. Alan Lightman, *Einstein's Dreams*, Pantheon Books, New York, 1993, p. 102.
8. Anna Hamilton Phelan, interview by William Froug, ed., *The New Screenwriter Looks at the New Screenwriter*, Silman-James Press, Los Angeles, 1991, p. 35.
9. Perl, Sondra, "Understanding Composing," *To Compose: Teaching Writing in High School and College*, Heinemann, Portsmouth, New Hampshire, 1990, p. 196.
10. Joel and Ethan Coen, *Blood Simple*, St. Martin's Press, New York, 1988, p. x.

3

Creative Problem Solving

Some problems are just too complicated for rational, logical solutions. They admit of insights, not answers.[1]

—Jerome Wiesner

When you create, you pluck ideas from thin air, imbue characters with living spirits, spin scenes into layers of meaning, and write until your mind is numb. Yet creating isn't limited to breathing life into stories or writing long past dark; creating is also problem-solving.

When you imagine a problem-solver, what type of person comes to mind? Perhaps it's a researcher in a white lab coat stooping over a microscope. Maybe it's a plumber twisting uncomfortably beneath the kitchen sink, or a parent bandaging the bloody knee of a teary-eyed toddler. Chances are you don't envision a composer poking at the piano keys in search of a melody, a sculptor chipping away at the marble in search of definition, or a scriptwriter rearranging words on a page in search of a story.

Problem-solving is usually not associated with artists. One of my former students, Diane Dutra, identified her confusion about artists as problem-solvers in her journal entry.

> Maybe I'm a mathematician and not an artist. Give me a problem to solve. I may not solve it correctly, but in the face of absurdity I may come up with an equally absurd answer. Mathematicians solve problems, answer questions. Artists make up the problems, and ask the questions.

Diane's thinking is very astute, and absolutely correct. Artists provoke us to question our own perceptions and to confront the complexities and

ambiguities of life. This, however, does not preclude artists from having to solve problems, nor does it address the fact that artists must know what questions to ask of themselves.

Diane suggests that in the face of absurdity, an absurd answer may be the solution. Her instincts are right again. Sometimes the only answer to a problem can be found in the realm of the absurd. Embrace the absurd. Even if it doesn't satisfy your questions, it'll remind you to laugh from time to time.

Later in her entry, Diane expressed her concern about what questions to ask.

> So creating a story is a problem. Why can't I solve it? Maybe I don't know the questions. In all the years of schooling and reality I don't remember ever being taught how to question.

Actually, Diane knows how to question far better than she realizes. In her thinking, she is formulating internal questions like: "how do artists solve problems?," "how do you create a story?" and "how do you know what questions to ask?" By shaping the questions, Diane is already beginning to puzzle through the answers. Diane has discovered that the questions you ask determine the answers you find, and ultimately, the strategies for solving problems. Learning to formulate your own questions is essential in the artistic process.

THE ART OF QUESTIONING

Whenever possible, ask new questions—questions you've never considered in the past. Turn the words around in the question so you're forced to rethink it. Instead of asking, "what would happen if a young girl grew old very rapidly?" ask yourself, "what would happen if an old woman grew young very rapidly?" Play with the elements of the question. Don't get locked into an answer too quickly.

If you don't feel you have enough experience formulating questions, consider the model for questioning designed by Ken Styles and Gray Cavanagh. They identify four levels of questioning and thinking: factual, convergent, divergent, and judgmental.[2] These levels can provide a framework to guide you as you formulate questions during the writing process.

When you begin to develop a story, ask yourself simple, direct questions that require **factual thinking**. Who is the story about? Where does the story take place? When does the story take place? These straightforward questions should be the easiest to answer.

Other, perhaps more difficult, questions may emerge as you work. For instance, what is the central issue or heart of your story? To discover the answer, you may need to consider a variety of possible solutions. All of these possibilities then converge into a satisfactory answer. This **convergent thinking** requires that your answer be the result of constructing different questions to find one acceptable answer.

To discover the central issue or heart of the story you will probably want to go back to the source of the story. What is the source of your story? Why did this idea interest you? Why did this idea persist over all others? If you had to single out the truth of the story, how would you articulate that truth? If you had to distill all the language of the story into one word, what would that word be? Keep posing and reposing questions, and eventually you'll discover a satisfactory answer.

Part of the problem with asking questions is the expectation that there is only one acceptable answer. Yet oftentimes, many valid answers may be attained by formulating a variety of questions. **Divergent thinking** introduces that possibility. Consider this question: What do you expect to learn by writing this story?

In order to discover the varied answers to this question, you'll need to pose more questions. For instance, of all the stories that you might choose to tell, why is it important for you to tell this story? What do you think you'll learn about yourself by writing this story? What do you hope to learn about scriptwriting by writing this story? Is it necessary to learn anything during the writing process? You will probably come up with numerous answers, any and all of which are legitimate responses.

The last kind of questioning you might consider involves **judgmental thinking**, which requires that you reach your answers by making judgments and formulating opinions. Perhaps you're wondering, "IS there a marketplace for my story?" You might answer this by formulating an opinion based on your knowledge of popular genres, box office statistics, and marketing strategies.

Be aware that this is a difficult question to answer and that the answer will always be opinion rather than fact. Many a producer has tried to answer this question unsuccessfully. Remember *Heaven's Gate, Ishtar, The Last Action Hero, Cutthroat Island, Waterworld*, and *The Avengers*? The fact is, there's almost no reliable method of predicting the marketplace. As William Goldman so aptly stated, "Nobody knows anything."[3] If this is true, then you might want to rethink your question. Perhaps you should instead be asking yourself, "what story do I want to see on the screen?" or "how do I want the audience to respond to my story?"

It's also important to remember that answers may not be evident right away. You may not know the answers to some of your questions until you've finished the story. Writers often don't know the theme when they begin writing, but it may rise to the top like cream once they've finished.

In the following excerpt, Daniel Pyne (*Doc Hollywood, Pacific Heights, The Hard Way, White Sands, The People*, and *Where's Marlow*), discusses how difficult it is for him to discover the core of the story.

> But, let's see, the hardest thing for me is finding the simple core of the story, what it's really about. Sometimes I don't find it until I'm working with the director and we're going through and polishing, and the director figures it out. I think as a writer you have an idea, and then you complicate it. You layer it and layer it, and you make a screenplay out of it. It's a wonderful piece, but you're unconscious now of what the core was, what you were really inspired to write about. But when you go to make the movie, you've got to be able to explain to everybody on the movie, from the director on down, what that core idea was so that they can see where you started. You have to strip it all back away.[4]

If you don't have the answers to the questions, be patient with yourself. Part of what drives artists to create a single work or a body of work are the questions that they continue to ask themselves and their audiences. Think of the filmmakers you admire. Do they have any dominant or reoccurring themes in their work? If so, they're probably searching for answers through their own work or their work is providing a framework for their questioning.

List the films that have influenced you. Why were you drawn to these stories? Did they explore similar themes? Do you often gravitate toward the work of the same filmmakers?

It's four hundred years from now. Another writer who has always admired your work is writing a book about you. Think of the story for which you most want to be remembered, the story that best represents you as a writer. Describe that story.

One of the classic questions writers ask is the open-ended "what if . . . ?" What if . . . Scarlett O'Hara and Rhett Butler were reincarnated as different people in another life? What if . . . an alien force blocked out all the television screens in the world? What if . . . someone slipped a magic potion in a city's water supply that mesmerized everyone in the town, inspiring them to love one other? The "what if?" question works because it opens up countless possibilities. When you come to a place in your story that you can't seem to get past, ask yourself "what if . . . ?"

What if you want to write a script about a mermaid who finds herself in a big city and falls in love with a man? Sound familiar? You're right— it's *Splash*, a literal "fish out of water" story. What if you didn't know there had already been a movie made about this idea?

ANTICIPATING PROBLEMS

One of the best ways to solve problems is to anticipate them. You need to research your ideas *before* you begin writing, unless you'd like to spend months of your life writing a story that's so similar to an already produced film that you'll never be able to see your story on the screen.

How do you research ideas? Read fairy tales, poems, short stories, novels, periodicals, newspapers—anything you can get your hands on. Familiarize yourself with films, past and present. Read books about films. Take a class in film appreciation or film history. Watch films on television. Frequent movie theatres. Read scripts.

Writers of scripts need to be readers of scripts. Scripts familiarize you with scriptwriting, inform you of previously produced stories, serve as models for problem-solving, and introduce you to format conventions and style.

For some curious, elusive reason, it rarely occurs to novice scriptwriters that it might be a good idea to read a script or two. Would you aspire to be a poet or novelist without ever having read a poem or novel?

If you have an idea for a script that is based on a real person or event, you'll need to research your subject more extensively. Genuine research requires devotion to your subject, multiple sources, and a great deal of time. For instance, when John Sayles, one of America's foremost independent filmmakers, researched *Eight Men Out*, he consulted diverse sources and devoted many years to the preparation of the script.

> I did quite a bit of research. I read about the Boston police strike. I had already been doing labor history which eventually turned into *Matewan*. I read a lot of the Chicago writers who grew up in that period. In order to get a better feeling for the dialogue of the time, I read a lot of Ring Lardner, James T. Farrell and Nelson Algren—people who were writing fiction in the thirties based on the characters they grew up with in the twenties. I read Dos Passos's *1919*. I read anything that had to do with baseball and gangsters in that era, from Elliot Ness books to *The Rise and Fall of the Jewish Gangster in America*. I learned that sociology was born in the Chicago of the twenties. It's probably the best documented city in the country, even better than New York City. Carl Sandburg, for instance, covered the big race riot that happened in 1920. Those documents are still around. *Eight Men Out* wasn't the first screenplay I ever wrote, but it did take twelve years to get to the screen.[5]

Whether it takes you twelve hours or twelve years, you need to be sure you've researched your subject well enough that you're able to write your story confidently.

RESPONDING TO WORKS IN PROGRESS

One of the most difficult problems you may encounter as a writer is isolation. Unless you have a writing partner or are part of a team of writers, you'll probably feel more and more alone as you write. Progressively, you begin to feel as if you're sinking deeper and deeper into a black hole of isolation from which you'll never emerge.

Aside from the pervasive loneliness of the endeavor, the biggest disadvantage of writing is having no one to respond to your work-in-progress. It's nearly impossible for you to objectively critique your own work. Annie Dillard eloquently articulated the problem in her book, *The Writing Life*.

> Another luxury for the imagination is the writer's own feeling about the work. There is neither a proportional relationship, nor an inverse one, between a writer's estimation of a work in progress and its actual quality. The feeling that the work is magnificent, and the feeling that it is abominable, are both mosquitoes to be repelled, ignored, or killed, but not indulged.[6]

So what do you do? How do you know if your story is engaging? What do you do when you're blocked? What if you have identified the problem but you don't know how to solve it? The answer is simple—ask. But whom do you ask?

The most ideal respondent would be a professional scriptwriter. It's unlikely that you would have the opportunity to receive feedback from a working scriptwriter, but professional writers and writing services who provide script analyses are available.

There are limitations to utilizing these services. Usually, these individuals and services provide written response to completed scripts, not works-in-progress. This prohibits you from having a dialogue with the reader or from receiving feedback to a work-in-progress. Also, reader's fees may be substantial, ranging upward of one hundred dollars per script. Additionally, you'd need to research the credentials of the individual or service. While many of them are legitimate, an equal or greater number of charlatans infest the field. If you decide to consult with a professional or service, be sure to request references or credentials.

Is it advisable to ask a friend, parent, or lover? Probably not. People who love you generally respond glowingly to your work. It's not so much that they're adept liars; it's just that they harbor this secret knowledge—

that you are a genius beyond reproach. Of course, there are always exceptions—if your mother is a Pulitzer-prize-winning author, ask away.

Whomever you ask, make sure that person is someone you trust and
respect, someone well read who has an understanding of a good story.
Credentials aren't necessary—honesty, intelligence, and insight are. Ask
another writer, a teacher, a librarian, or a colleague. Ask your car mechanic
if you trust that person's sensibilities. Chuck Palahuniuk, author of the
novel *Fight Club* (which was adapted into a film), wrote the novel when he
was working as a diesel mechanic. He even wrote parts of the novel from
under a diesel truck.

If you have an earnest respondent who has limited experience responding to works-in-progress, you might find a **conference** with a respondent
beneficial. Conferencing helps you and your respondent focus on specific
areas of concentration within the work-in-progress. In preparation for the
conference, you both might find these guidelines helpful.

GUIDELINES FOR CONFERENCING

To the respondent
- Before evaluating the script, ask questions of the writer. Are there
  specific areas of concern of which you should be aware?
- Ask the writer if it's appropriate for you to write comments
  directly on the script.
- Be aware of your own biases: If you hate fantasy and the script
  is a fantasy, let the writer know your comments may have an
  inherent bias.
- Take notes so you remember what you want to discuss during the
  conference.
- Be honest, evaluating as carefully and objectively as possible.
- Don't forget to praise the outstanding qualities of the script.
- Structure your comments; you may want to respond to uniqueness, theme, tone, format, plot, structure (continuity, logic, pro-
  gression of scenes, accuracy of details), characterization, and
  dialogue.
- Be specific. Avoid vague or broad answers and, whenever possible, suggest several possible solutions or alternatives to perceived
  problems.
- Organize your notes before conferencing with the scriptwriter so
  that your comments are logical and focused.

To the scriptwriter
- Before the respondent evaluates your script, discuss any problems
  that you're having with the script and ask for specific comments
  on those areas.

- Let the respondent know if it's all right to write comments directly on the script.

- Be aware that the respondent may have biases and that all responses are subjective, no matter how objective the respondent tries to be.

- Take notes when a respondent is conferencing with you so you don't forget specific suggestions later.

- Be sure to ask for clarification if a respondent's comments are unclear.

- Try to avoid being oversensitive; remember that a respondent is there to support your efforts.

- Try not to react immediately to criticism; think about the respondent's comments for awhile before reacting.

- Try to be open to suggestions; the respondent may suggest an idea that solves a problem or adds needed life to your script.

- Remember that the respondent is not infallible; any solutions offered by the respondent may not be the right answer for you—trust your own instincts.

- Remember that the script is yours; a respondent makes suggestions but you make the decisions—no one should tell you what artistic choices to make.

- Thank your respondent for the effort; it's a sensitive task with limited rewards.

Once you've had a conference with your respondent, take some time to sift through the suggestions and see what makes sense to you. If you're really resistant to a suggestion, you need to ask yourself why you're resisting so strongly. It may mean that you considered that suggestion prior to the conference and have already ruled it out. More than likely, if the suggestion really irritates you, the respondent may have struck a chord of truth.

If you decide that the respondent is right, you need to puzzle through the problem and try to create a satisfactory solution. This solution may not be evident immediately. You may have to write ahead and come back to the problem later. You may choose to put the script aside for awhile and go back to it with "new eyes" later. Time is a wonderful distancing device that enables you to return to your work with newfound objectivity.

Based on the respondent's comments, you may also decide that a scene or character is unnecessary. One of the most painful moments you'll have as a writer is the realization that it's necessary to cut out a scene or character that you absolutely love. Take heart—somehow those scenes or characters insinuate their way into future scripts. Even if you never use them again, don't forget that you had fun creating them and that's part of the joy of writing.

If you aren't able to find a respondent or you want further commentary, you might also consider a **cold reading**. A cold reading is a reading of the script by readers who are reading it "cold"; that is, they haven't had much exposure to the script prior to the reading. The advantage to a cold reading is that you can hear the dialogue delivered aloud. When you listen to dialogue, you may have a totally different response than when you read the dialogue silently to yourself.

If you have community or professional theatre available where you live, you may be able to induce some actors to read for you. If you don't feel confident enough to approach actors, ask your friends. If need be, bribe them with promises of food or drink, preferably after the reading.

Be sure that you set the right tone for the reading. Explain that this is a work-in-progress and the purpose of the reading is to help you develop your work. If your script is a serious drama, treat your readers as serious participants. If your script is a comedy, try loosening up your readers before the reading.

It's important that you abstain from participating directly in the reading. You need to be free to listen to the dialogue and take notes as the reading progresses. Don't be afraid to interrupt and ask your readers to reread a portion of the script if necessary.

There are some disadvantages to a cold reading. Readers are usually not professional, rehearsed actors capable of fully interpreting the characters' roles. Dialogue that is well written may sound flat or ineffectual if read poorly. Also, if you schedule a reading too early in the progress of your work, you may find the process discouraging. If you're dissatisfied with the reading, you may become too critical of your work. If this happens, a kind of creative paralysis may overtake you, prohibiting you from returning to your work or convincing you that you need to start over again. It's wise to wait until a first draft or a substantial portion of your script is complete before you have a cold reading.

Think of the word "cold." What does it connote for you? Do you think of being sick with a cold or living in a cold climate? Have you ever known a cold person? Can you imagine how cold feels? Have you ever taken a cold shower or gone for a swim in icy cold water? Do you have any memories or experiences that you associate with cold? If you could live anywhere you wanted, would you live in a cold place? If so, where would it be? Describe it. If you dislike cold, why? What is it about cold you don't like?

The more you write, the more confidence you'll gain, enabling you to creatively solve the problems before you. Learning to question, anticipating

problems, and finding respondents to your work are some of the strategies that may help you solve problems. You'll learn more strategies in the next chapter as you begin to shape your ideas into the skeleton of a story.

REFERENCES

1. John-Roger and Peter McWilliams, *The Portable Life 101*, Prelude Press, Los Angeles, 1992, p. 34. Original source not cited.
2. Ken Styles and Gray Cavanagh, "Language Across the Curriculum: The Art of Questioning and Responding," *English Journal*, February 1980, p. 26.
3. William Goldman, *Adventures in the Screen Trade: A Personal View of Hollywood and Screenwriting*, Warner Books, New York, 1984, p. 39.
4. William Froug, *The New Screenwriter Looks at the New Screenwriter*, Silman-James Press, Los Angeles, 1991, p. 136.
5. George Hickenlooper, *Reel Conversations: Candid Interviews with Film's Foremost Directors and Critics*, Carol Publishing Group, New York, 1991, p. 304.
6. Annie Dillard, *The Writing Life*, Harper Perennial, New York, 1989, p. 15.

4

Bold Beginnings

Whatever you can do, or dream you can, begin it. Boldness has genius, power and magic in it.[1]

—Goethe

Perhaps the most daunting problem for writers is making the first move—not just the physical movement, the act of raising the hand to write, but the soulful act of moving inward. Where do you find the courage to begin?

In her spare but wise book, *The Writing Life*, Annie Dillard shares a story, originally told by Ernest Seton, that answers the question, "How do you begin?"

> You may wonder how you start, how you catch the first one. What do you use for bait?
>
> You have no choice. One bad winter in the Arctic, and not too long ago, an Algonquin woman and her baby were left alone after everyone else in their winter camp had starved. Ernest Thompson Seton tells it. The woman walked from the camp where everyone had died, and found at a lake a cache. The cache contained one small fishhook. It was simple to rig a line, but she had no bait, and no hope of bait. The baby cried. She took a knife and cut a strip from her own thigh. She fished with the worm of her own flesh and caught a jackfish; she fed the child and herself. Of course she saved the fish gut for bait. She lived alone at the lake, on fish, until spring, when she walked out again and found people. Seton's informant had seen the scar on her thigh.[2]

The story of the Algonquin woman is a metaphor representing the barren landscape every writer encounters in the beginning. You stand in the cold, search the horizon for an answer, and look within for the bait.

59

Only you have the substance necessary to begin and, ultimately, to sustain the writing. What do you have within you that you may call upon, that you may beckon to the telling?

Have you ever gone fishing? If so, do you have any memories associated with fishing? If you could fish for a memory, what would you use for bait? Scents or songs make juicy bait. If you could "catch" a memory that has eluded you, what memory would you snag? Do you believe memory is selective; that is, does your memory choose to remember some moments and elect to ignore others?

THE BECKONING

Have you ever heard the expression "gather your wits about you"? Its meaning implies a summoning of intellect and strength. When you think about it literally, its meaning is almost comical. It's as if you could herd stray bits of wisdom, like errant sheep, into a sensible mass. This thinking implies that it's a simple matter of summoning your thoughts and forcing them to respond at will.

Certainly thoughts can be controlled, but as you begin to move from concept to story, you may be better served giving your initial thoughts free rein. If you allow your seminal thoughts to spill forth, you'll be more likely to tap into the vast wealth of thoughts, emotions, and impressions residing in your subconscious.

Every writer devises methods for beckoning the mysteries of the subconscious. Spalding Gray, who's scripted feature-length monologues for the films *Swimming to Cambodia*, *Monster in a Box*, and *Gray's Anatomy*, shares how he makes sense of the stirrings of the subconscious.

> I see life as chaos essentially and then the structure is in trying to put the puzzle together. So right now, next to my desk in New York, I have a cardboard box. And I throw everything that's unanswered, disturbing or relevant to some of the things I'm thinking about, into that box. Then, when I have some time, maybe a year later, I'll dump it out and begin to put together the puzzle of a new monologue. I will take a spiral notebook and make an outline of progressive anecdotes, of stories that I think apply to the puzzle. So I begin to have a new take on my life, on where I am historically. What I'm thinking about. How I'm interacting with people. It grows out of a series of anecdotes. Then I begin to see the common theme by speaking it.[3]

Patterns or themes often emerge during the beckoning. In his book *Zen in the Art of Writing*, Ray Bradbury, a revered novelist, master of science fiction, and scriptwriter of *Moby Dick* (co-authored with John Huston), describes a systematic approach to beginning that he conceived in his early writing years. This approach allows patterns to emerge spontaneously.

> [But] along through those years I began to make lists of titles, to put down long lines of *nouns*. These lists were the provocations, finally, that caused my better stuff to surface. I was feeling my way toward something honest, hidden under the trapdoor on the top of my skull.
>
> The list ran something like this:
>
> THE LAKE. THE NIGHT. THE CRICKETS. THE RAVINE. THE ATTIC. THE BASEMENT. THE TRAPDOOR. THE BABY. THE CROWD. THE NIGHT TRAIN. THE FOG HORN. THE SCYTHE. THE CARNIVAL. THE CAROUSEL. THE DWARF. THE MIRROR MAZE. THE SKELETON.
>
> I was beginning to see a pattern in the list, in these words that I had simply flung forth on the paper, trusting my subconscious to give bread, as it were, to the birds.
>
> Glancing over the list, I discovered my old love and fright having to do with circuses and carnivals. I remembered, and then forgot, and then remembered again, how terrified I had been when my mother took me for my first ride on a merry-go-round. With the calliope screaming and the world spinning and the terrible horses leaping, I added my shrieks to the din. I did not go near the carousel again for years. When I really did, decades later, it rode me into the midst of *Something Wicked This Way Comes*.[4]

The simple lists that Bradbury generated became the spine of a story that was later published as fiction and produced as a film.

Write a list of your own. If you can't think of any words, try using nouns such as promises, lies, wishes, whispers, dreams, and nightmares to get you started. If that doesn't work, write lists of family and friends. How about listing places you've worked, places you've been, or places where you want to travel? Inventory things you've lost or things that have fallen apart. Do you have trunks or filing cabinets full of memorabilia? List their contents. The idea is to dust the cobwebs from the attic of your mind and get started.

Clustering is another strategy for discovering ideas, patterns, and themes. In her book *Writing the Natural Way*, Gabriele Lusser Rico describes clustering.

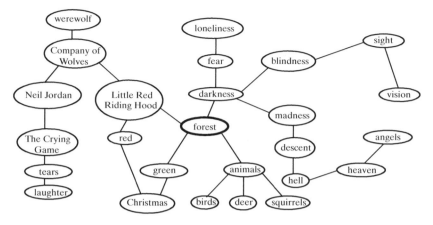

Figure 4.1

> Clustering is a nonlinear brainstorming process akin to free associa-
> tion. . . . It is the writing tool that accepts wondering, not knowing,
> seeming chaos, gradually mapping an interior landscape as ideas begin to
> emerge.[5]

To cluster, you start with a nuclear word that acts as a stimulus to generate ideas. As ideas emerge, cluster them around the nuclear word, attach-
ing stems between groupings of thought as pictured in Figure 4.1. You'll
be amazed at the patterns that emerge.

Once you've clustered, you may want to take one of the words or patterns and use that as a catalyst for further clustering. Cluster as often as
you like until you find the skeleton of a story.

A story may be sparked by a real event in your life or simply by observation. A real event often triggers the idea for an imagined incident. If you've
witnessed an event that shocked or touched you, it may be the impetus for
your script. Take some notes on your memory of the event. If there's any
documentation of what happened, compare the evidence to your memory.
Is your memory of the experience accurate? Maybe your memory has
embellished the event over time. Why do you think you remember this particular happening? Why do you want to tell a story based on this happening?
The questions you ask in your notes should help you find the core of a story.

Maybe you've been haunted by a place from your past. One way to
return to that place and to your past is by entering that world through a
story. To help you begin, you can physically return to the place. If that's
impossible, look at pictures of the place or research its history. Oral histories provide fresh insight into the past. Is there anyone associated with the
place who might be able to share stories about it? If so, you might want to
record a conversation with that person so you can retain all of the details,

or email that person specific questions. As you uncover the mystery of the place, of why it haunts you, you'll be able to move forward with a story. Even if the answers aren't clear, you should start writing. Maybe the reason you need to write this particular story is to slide inside the mystery and discover the answers from within.

Have you ever dreamed of a fantastic, imaginary world? If you can draw, you might actually want to sketch, color, or paint your vision of this world. In preparation for his film, *Ran*, Akira Kurosawa created a series of paintings revealing various scenes he'd envisioned. You don't need a brush to paint your vision; however, you can paint with words. In your journal, describe everything about your imagined world that your mind's eye sees. As you bring this world to life, you'll be led to the story.

You may find yourself following a character into the story. Characters may manifest themselves on a bus, at the market, at your family reunion—anywhere. Sometimes characters are inspired by real people, perhaps even by your enemies. In her book, *The Artist's Way*, Julia Cameron, an award-winning journalist, independent and documentary producer, and film and television writer, suggests that you create a monster hall of fame.[6] These monsters are not literal monsters; they're past enemies who have attacked your creative self-worth. Whose portraits would you hang in your monster hall of fame? If you had a hall of fame of heroes, whom would you include? Think of those people who have inspired you and those who have put obstacles in your path. Describe them in your journal. Unless your story is true, you won't want to use these people as characters, but you may want to incorporate some of their characteristics into the characters you create.

As you are led to the story by a happening, place, or character, jot down notes so you don't lose the inspiration or any significant details. If you don't have your journal or a notebook with you, write on the back of an old grocery list, a receipt, an envelope—anything handy.

It's a good idea to keep an idea file of notes, newspaper clippings, quotes, letters, or any other sources you've gathered. Whenever you feel uninspired, dig out your idea file and see what story might be beckoning you. As your idea file accumulates, you may discover patterns, themes, and, in some cases, hints of synchronicity.

Have you ever had an experience that seems to be mystically linked to another experience? Carl Jung identified the concept of **synchronicity** as a "meaningful coincidence" that appears on the surface to be accidentally or coincidentally related but may have a deeper significance.[7] The premise of *Sleepless in Seattle* is founded on synchronicity. If Annie (Meg Ryan) hadn't heard Sam (Tom Hanks) on the talk show, they would never have been brought together. Their "meeting" over the radio is not accidental; it's a meaningful coincidence.

Synchronicity occurs when you recognize a connection between events or when an outer event mirrors an inner dream or process. Even if you can't

articulate what these connections represent, they may have meaning for you. In her book, *Writing from the Inner Self*, Elaine Farris Hughes helps you discover meaning through a series of questions: "How much time lapsed between the events? In what ways were the different events parallel? What kind of meaning tied them together in your mind?"[8] The goal is to discern how these separate events might be related and what meaning they may hold for you.

All of these methods will enable you to bridge your subconscious musings with your conscious goals to tell a good story. Whether you borrow from other writers' suggestions or invent your own strategies, it's important that you experiment until you discover what works for you.

As your ideas rise to the surface, it's important that you resist judging them. Judging your ideas as they're forming is intrusive to the creative process, a kind of self-censorship. What may seem like a dumb or silly idea at first, may become a fresh, inventive idea if you allow it to fully develop. Three of my former students, Mike Monello, Dan Myrick, and Eduardo Sanchez, pitched a vague idea in a class of mine. They weren't sure how they could do it but they knew what they wanted—to create a horror film with a documentary feel, something genuinely scary. They'd been influenced by the 80s television series *In Search Of* and wanted to create a film with a similar feel. They kept playing with the idea and refining it. Their idea became the foundation for *The Blair Witch Project*, one of the most successful independent films in cinema history.

If you have an abundance of ideas, you'll need to narrow them down to find the story worth telling. To narrow down your ideas, you have to create a kind of conceptual net. This net should let stale ideas through and catch fresh ones. How do you weave the net to catch the best ideas? Weave it with questions. Which idea is the most original? Which idea nags you, haunts you? Which idea creates a vision of the story on the screen? Which idea would be the most fun to develop? Which would be the most challenging? Which idea disturbs you the most? Which idea do you care about the most? Add your own questions. Once you've answered all the questions, see which idea satisfies the most questions.

If you're still unsure about what story to tell, reread some of your journal entries. Sometimes even a single word or phrase can provide the impetus for a story. If you don't feel you have enough raw material yet, try focused journal writing.

FOCUSED JOURNAL WRITING

By now, you should be comfortable writing in your journal. In addition to your responses and ramblings, you may want to use your journal to develop specific sensibilities as you begin writing.

A sensory journal focuses on your senses; its objective is to make you acutely aware of your senses. Here are some suggestions for sharpening your sensory skills.

Sight: Remember that when you watch a film, you're seeing the world through a filmic window that provides selective vision. To think visually, you need to imagine that you're looking through the camera's eye. In her book *The Screenplay: A Blend of Film Form and Content*, Margaret Mehring suggests that you take a blank piece of paper and cut out a frame three inches high and four inches wide.[9] Now hold up the paper and use the frame to help you imagine filmic space. What view do you see? What can't you see? Is what you can't see as important as what you can see? To establish varying points of view, look through the frame from various heights and angles. How do the varying points of view affect your perception of the world? Hold the frame still. Move it from side to side or up and down. Move it quickly, then slowly. Write down what you discover as you manipulate the world through the filmic window.

Sound: Sound in film can create ambience, mood, tension, and irony. In order to suggest how sound might be integrated into your story, you need to be aware of the sounds that surround you. In *The Listening Book*, W. A. Mathieu suggests that you write "symphonies" of sound and place:

> Get a pencil and paper. Become aware of all the sounds you are hearing now, this moment, as you read. Make a list of them. Close your eyes from time to time. Swivel your head slightly to change the mix. Make a sweep from nearby sounds to distant sounds. Fall into the distance. Become transparent. Now fall into the nearness. Make a sweep from the highest sounds to the lowest ones. Disappear into the stratosphere, reappear underground. If your space is quiet enough you will hear your own internal sounds: breathing, maybe your blood in your ears. Or the subtle sounds of cloth against cloth, skin against skin. Count everything; write everything down. Use words economically. Later, if you like, you can set the scene and go into detail.
>
> Now make your sweeps into scans so rapid that you have the illusion of hearing everything at once. Now close your eyes and hear everything at once. Now cup your hands behind your ears. Technicolor!
>
> This is the sound of your now, your Symphony of Place.[10]

Close your eyes and listen to the sounds around you. What do you hear? Right now I hear the click of my fingers on the keyboard, the barely discernible hum of the computer, the loud churn of the washer, the heavy knock of the tennis shoes in the dryer, the fitful drip of the water in the sink, the quick lick of my cat's tongue on her tail, and the muffled voice of my daughter singing behind her closed bedroom door. Quickly and painlessly, I've composed my Symphony #1. Now you try it.

Write your first symphony of sounds. Listen for pitch and loudness. Are the sounds synchronous or asynchronous, steady or intermittent, irritating or pleasant? Remember to number and date your symphony so that you can learn to become sensitive to different sounds at different times.

Touch: Part of the way that your characters will reveal themselves is through touch. In the film *The Miracle Worker*, when Helen Keller (portrayed by Patty Duke in her Oscar-winning performance) touches water and makes the conceptual connection between water as a physical property and water as an idea expressed in language, it is a startling and moving moment. You must be able to recognize differences in touch in order to imagine how your characters might respond to touch. How does touch change in relation to temperature? How do you visually show someone responding to extreme temperatures? Try taking off your shoes and walking on different surfaces. How would you show varying reactions to the different surfaces? Touch the inanimate objects in your present setting. Now touch a person or animal. How do the sensations of touching an object differ from those of touching a person or animal? What is pleasing about each of the experiences? What is displeasing? What happens when we deny ourselves intimacy with other humans? Reflect on these questions in your journal.

Smell: Your characters will be more credible if they respond to all the sensations of the world in a realistic manner. The sense of smell can reveal the beautiful and the ugly. How much will your characters rely on smell? What if one of your characters were unable to smell? To heighten your awareness of smell, go to a farmer's market, carnival, county fair, or flea market. As you pass by the booths and stalls, what do you smell? Do the smells mingle, or are you able to discern distinct smells? Are the smells pleasant or repulsive? Think of other places you've been. How do city smells differ from country smells? How do inside smells differ from outside smells? How does the smell of a hospital differ from that of a warehouse or a home? How do smells change when the weather changes? How does the smell of animal fur compare to that of human flesh? Write about the way in which smells affect you and about any strong associations you have based on smell.

Taste: Taste can be shown through the reactions of your characters. In *Big*, when Josh (Tom Hanks) takes a hefty gulp of caviar, he reacts by wincing painfully before he spews it out. Even though the viewers can't taste the caviar, we can imagine how it tastes from Josh's reaction. List the foods that might make someone wince. Obvious choices are lemon or onion, for instance. You may be repulsed by foods that some of your friends eat or by foods that other ethnic groups prefer. Have you ever eaten something that actually tasted good until you found out what it was?

Some people have an aversion to eating foods from anatomical parts such as brains or intestines. List the foods that you don't ever think you'd have the courage to taste. Why did you list those particular foods? List the foods that you love and describe how they taste. What have you tasted that isn't related to food? Have you ever tasted snow, mud, rain, or dust? How about a teardrop? Is taste important to you? What if you couldn't taste anything—would that be a blessing or a curse? The next time you sit down to eat a meal, slow down and concentrate on the sensations that you experience as you eat. Write about your reactions in your journal.

Another example of a focused journal is the dream journal. A dream journal is a place to record and reflect upon your waking and sleeping dreams. You won't find a dream journal to be of much use unless you believe that dreams are significant.

Writers often express a reliance on dreams to help them foster their work and address concerns. Anne Rice, author of *Interview with the Vampire* and the series of books known as the Vampire Chronicles, feels that daydreams have a direct relationship to her writing.

> I'm a very heavy daydreamer. I have been since I was a child. To me daydreaming is intimately connected with writing. Writing is like daydreaming. It's putting down in dramatic form whatever is on your mind. Daydreams are some sort of code for whatever concerns you. I really can't imagine what the minds are like of those who can't daydream or fantasize because I'm so used to doing it. So, my writing grew out of that obviously.[11]

If you write down your daydreams, you may discover the impetus for a story within your dreams. If you record daydreams over a period of time, patterns and themes may become evident. It's a good idea to write down your daydreams as soon after they occur as possible, while the dream is fresh in your mind.

What if you're not much of a daydreamer? Consider keeping a journal of your night dreams. Night dreams may have an even greater influence than daydreams on your writing. In *Writers Dreaming*, John Sayles discusses a series of dreams that helped shape one of his films. Read the description of this dream and see if you can determine which film grew out of the dream.

> It was a kind of sunny day and I was on a street in Harlem. It was a black neighborhood and I said to myself, Oh, this is Harlem, I recognize the buildings. I was watching this black man walk down the street. He was obviously a little bit frightened and he looked really lost. Then I realized—the way you realize things in dreams without seeing anything dramatized, or anybody saying anything—that, Oh, he's from another planet. No wonder he feels lost. He can't talk. How alienating, literally, that must be. How lonely he must be.[12]

If you're familiar with John Sayles' work, you've probably guessed the answer. This dream, mingled with a few dreams that preceded it, shaped the story for what would become *Brother from Another Planet*. Although Sayles' work isn't usually influenced by his dreams, in this particular instance there was a direct connection between his film and his dreams.

Night dreams are not only rich resources as you begin to shape your story, they are also valuable resources during the writing process. Writers frequently rely on dreams to help them solve problems as the story unfolds. One of my former students, Michael Ozias, wrote of a dream he had that helped him struggle through a feature-length script he was assigned in a former class.

> One night, after working on it (the script) very intensely, I had a peculiar dream. I dreamt that I was standing before a crumpled sheet of metal, roughly my own height, and I had to make a mirror out of it with a sledgehammer. At first, I looked at it and saw only fragmented images, hints of pieces representing a whole. So, I began pounding away. Slowly but surely, it began to take shape. The image was becoming clearer.
>
> Occasionally, however, I would hit it too hard, in which case I would have to approach it from the other side and hit it again. After hours of blood, sweat and tears I had finally flattened it out. I then had only to polish it and be done.
>
> I woke disturbed. At first I couldn't remember the dream, but when I finally did it began gnawing at me. I wanted to know what it meant. A day later, I sat down to write and suddenly it was all so clear. The sheet of metal was my script. Originally, it was a jumbled set of fragmented ideas. But after laboring intensely, the fragments formed a whole. I then polished and refined it to have my finished product. It now formed a complete image—an image of myself.

Amy Tan, author of the novel *The Joy Luck Club* and co-author of the script, discussed how dreams have helped her with story endings.

> Sometimes, if I'm stuck on the ending of a story, I'll just take the story with me to bed. I'll let it become part of a dream and see if something surfaces.
>
> I did this once with a story in *The Joy Luck Club*, the one about a woman trying to get out of an arranged marriage. As I was writing it, I felt as though I was blocking myself into a corner. I was like a little rat running around a maze and I didn't know how to get out. This woman in the story was in a complicated situation. She couldn't break her promise, yet she needed to get out of the marriage. So I took that story problem to bed with me, along with some other information, and I dreamed an ending that turned out to be quite workable and funny.

I don't normally see my characters in dreams exactly as they appear in a book, but I do experience a similar kind of feeling or emotion, something that gives me new insight into the questions that I'm asking of those characters.[13]

If you feel a dream journal might be helpful to you, keep your journal by your bed, and make sure there's a pen nearby. It's essential that you write down all you can remember of your dreams as soon as you wake up. If you let too much time pass, you may lose details that are relevant to the significance of the dream.

Do you believe dreams are important? Do you daydream? If so, what are some of your most daring daydreams? How were dreams treated in your family? Were they dismissed as meaningless, imaginative folly, revered as signifiers from the subconscious, or regarded as an inexplicable curiosity? Though research tells us that everyone dreams, some people are unable to remember their night dreams. Do you remember your dreams? If so, are they hazy outlines of memory or do you remember vivid details? Do you remember any of the dreams of your childhood? Have you ever had a dream that disturbed you so deeply that it lingered in your mind for days or weeks? Have you ever had a reoccurring dream? If so, why do you think that specific dream reoccurred? Have you ever tried to consciously prepare yourself before sleep to meet the challenge of the dream when you enter the dream state? Fyodor Dostoyevsky wrote, "They tease me now, telling me it was only a dream. But does it matter whether it was a dream or reality, if the dream made known to me the truth?"[14] Do you think dreams harbor truths?

To be a scriptwriter, it helps to be a dreamer. Not only will you draw ideas from your dreams, your dreams will sustain you through the arduous task of writing a script.

All of the ideas presented in this chapter demonstrate various methods that writers have employed to help them get started. As you develop your thoughts, you may want to experiment with these strategies or devise some of your own. If none of these methods works for you, invent some of your own. Be playful. Eventually, you'll find what works for you.

Now that you have an awareness of the creative process, you're ready to proceed to the professional aspects of scriptwriting. In Part Two, you'll learn how to take your ideas, shape them into stories, and write them in script format. Part Two will also cover aspects of professional scriptwriting such as adaptation, the ethics of scriptwriting, and suggestions for marketing your script.

REFERENCES

1. John-Roger and Peter McWilliams, *The Portable Life 101*, Prelude Press, Los Angeles, 1992, p. 105. Original source not cited.
2. Annie Dillard, *The Writing Life*, Harper Perennial, New York, 1989, pp. 12–13.
3. Naomi Epel, ed., *Writers Dreaming*, Carol Southern Books, New York, 1993, pp. 82–83.
4. Ray Bradbury, *Zen in the Art of Writing*, Bantam Book, New York, 1990, pp. 17–18.
5. Gabriele Lusser Rico, *Writing the Natural Way: Using Right-Brain Techniques to Release Your Expressive Powers*, J. P. Tarcher, Inc., Los Angeles, 1983, pp. 28–29.
6. Julia Cameron, *The Artist's Way: A Spiritual Path to Higher Creativity*, Jeremy P. Tarcher/Perigree Books, Los Angeles, 1992, p. 38.
7. Carl G. Jung and M.- L. von Franz, *Man and His Symbols*, Dell Publishing, New York, 1964, p. 226.
8. Elaine Farris Hughes, *Writing from the Inner Self*, Harper Perennial, New York, 1991, pp. 106–107.
9. Margaret Mehring, *The Screenplay: A Blend of Film Form and Content*, Focal Press, Boston, 1990, p. 19.
10. W. A. Mathieu, *The Listening Book: Discovering Your Own Music*, Shambhala, Boston, 1991, pp. 10–11.
11. Epel, p. 210.
12. Epel, p. 221.
13. Epel, p. 285.
14. Laynee Wild, *The Complete Dream Journal*, Pomegranate Artbooks, San Francisco, 1992, p. 19. Original source not cited.

PART II

The Professional Process

5

Becoming a Professional

You can't go to work! You have to stay home and write!
— Henry (Thomas Jay Ryan) from *Henry Fool*[1]

When you imagine yourself as a scriptwriter, what do you see yourself doing? Are you drinking wine at a trendy café, your fingers flying on your PalmPilot as you nail down the next deal with your agent on your cell phone? Perhaps you've made that multi-million-dollar sale and you're shopping for a house in Malibu or a wicked red sports car—oh, why not just snatch them both up? Maybe you're dressed in evening clothes, nervously awaiting your Oscar for the Best Original Screenplay. Admit it, you've probably even composed a sample acceptance speech—just in case.

The reality of scriptwriting has very little to do with what you may have imagined. As a professional scriptwriter, you must establish goals, develop consistent work habits, familiarize yourself with related literature and resources, and present your work according to the standards established by the film industry.

Before you're able to establish goals, you must be clear about what your goals are. Goals differ dramatically from dreams. Dreams are merely idle imaginings if they're not acted upon. Goals enable you to act upon your dreams.

As a scriptwriter, what are your goals and dreams? Is there a correlation between them? How often do you write? Do you write consistently

85

or sporadically? Is there a time every day when you sit down to write? If not, how often do you write? If your work habits aren't established, how could you change your behavior to accommodate your writing? How important is it for you to be a scriptwriter? Would you be willing to give something up to become a scriptwriter? Are you willing to devote years to your craft if necessary? Imagine that it's ten years from now. What do you see yourself doing? Is writing a part of that scene? Write a futuristic scenario featuring you as the main character. Who have you become, and what are you doing with your life? Did you achieve your goals? If not, why not?

The questions posed in the prompt, and those you ask yourself, will help you determine the extent of your commitment. If you decide that you have what it takes, then you should begin by setting up a rigorous schedule for yourself.

Schedule time for writing on a regular basis. It helps to build a pleasant routine. Make yourself a cup of tea or some fresh juice before beginning. If you have a hectic home life, you might want to go elsewhere to write. Having an office, library, or retreat will help you concentrate on your script. If you don't have the luxury of a separate writing environment and you work at home, set your alarm and get up before everyone else. Use the quiet early hours to write. If you're not a morning person, wait until everyone goes to bed to begin writing. If you're too mentally tired at the end of the day, take a nap earlier to solve the problem. It helps to have lengthy blocks of time without interruption, but if that's not possible, invent a schedule that works for you. If your true desire is to be a scriptwriter, you'll find a way.

For the determined writer, words have a way of finding their way to light. Consider the story of this seventeen-year-old writer, as told in *The Writer's Home Companion*.

> Some authors have had to overcome more than writing blocks or a new word processor. Lady Jane Grey, for example, ruled as England's queen for nine days when Edward VI died. When Edward's half-sister, Mary I, took the throne away from her, she banished Lady Jane, only seventeen, to the Tower of London during her trial. She was offered a pardon if she renounced her faith and became a Catholic. She refused and was immediately beheaded. In her jail cell were found pieces of paper covered in tiny pinpricks. It was later discovered that, when held to the light, the marks formed verses she had composed before her death.[2]

Lady Grey carried her convictions and determination to her grave. You shouldn't need to test your resolve so dramatically but you do need to remain devoted to your goals.

When you arrange your schedule, be sure to allow time to read as well as to write. Scripts serve as superlative models for format, story, structure, character, and dialogue. In addition to scripts, you'll find an abundance of helpful books related to scriptwriting and the marketing of scripts. You should also read periodicals related to scriptwriting, filmmaking, and the film industry. In the back of this book, you'll find a guide that provides you with an annotated compilation of resources available to scriptwriters.

The hunger to learn should never be finite; education, like life, is a continuum. As a writer, you should welcome time to, in Ray Bradbury's words, "feed the Muse." Read anything that beckons you, whether it be a comic strip or an epic poem. Bradbury suggests a steady menu of essays, short stories, novels, and poetry. What should you read? What if you don't know anything about poetry, for instance? What poems should you read? Bradbury wisely advises:

> Any poetry that makes your hair stand up along your arms. Don't force yourself too hard. Take it easy. Over the years you may catch up to, move even with, and pass T. S. Eliot on your way to other pastures. You say you don't understand Dylan Thomas? Yes, but your ganglion does, and your secret wits, and all your unborn children. Read him, as you can read a horse with your eyes, set free and charging over an endless green meadow on a windy day.[3]

When you feed the Muse, don't neglect your other appetites. Remember that film is a collaborative medium that unites words, images, and sound. Your feast should also include a sumptuous array of paintings, sculptures, photographs, prints, sketches, etchings, cartoons—any visual delights. Listen, too, to your favorite symphony, opera, jazz, blues, rock, rap, rapping, tapping on the pots by the children in the kitchen, the sounds of sirens screaming through the streets, shutters banging on windows, the screen door snapping shut, the leaves crackling in a fire.

The Muse lurks in gardens, parks, rivers, oceans, mountains, valleys, trails, streets, junkyards, antique shops, museums, bookstores, libraries, universities—even in places you'd never suspect. The Muse may be closer than you think.

Suppose you were among a small group of people selected to travel in space. For your lengthy voyage, you're permitted to pack one book, one film, one painting, one photograph, and one musical composition. What personal treasures would you take? If you had had the same opportunity when you were ten years old, what do you think you would have taken then? What if you were to take that trip ten years from today? Do

you think you'd want to take the same items that you would take today? How much of the ten-year-old still exists within you? Do you think part of the essential you will remain intact throughout your life?

Once you've established a schedule for writing and feeding the Muse, you're ready to write your script. As you begin to shape your words into story form, you need to familiarize yourself with the conventions of scriptwriting.

FORMAT CONVENTIONS

No matter how powerful a story you've created, if you can't present it in professional script format, it will probably end up gathering dust on a shelf rather than landing on the desk of an agent or producer. The presentation of your script reflects your professionalism.

The conventions of scriptwriting allude to what is commonly accepted as professional script format within the film community. Though you will always be able to find exceptions to the rules, these generalities reflect the dominant practices employed by scriptwriters. You should also be aware that the conventions and style of scriptwriting have changed throughout the history of scriptwriting; what is the contemporary norm may evolve into something quite different five or ten years from now.

A good example of a recent change in format involves camera direction. Traditionally, feature film scripts included excessive camera direction. Today's prevailing wisdom is to avoid camera direction since it's the domain of the director, not the scriptwriter. Also, one of the goals of good storytelling is to totally engage the audience. Since the first audience of the script is the reader, the reader should be drawn into the story without being disengaged by superfluous camera direction. A well-written script implies direction by creating visual moments within the action with minimal or no camera direction.

Consider the implied direction in this sparely written scene from Stephan Elliott's script, *The Adventures of Priscilla Queen of the Desert*. In this excerpt, Adam (Guy Pearce) dressed as his drag queen persona, Felicia, rides atop a shabby silver bus affectionately donned Priscilla.

```
The red desert is flashing past to the accompaniment
of some very grand opera. Suddenly, FELICIA appears in
full frame, mouthing the Italian soprano in perfect
synchronization.

                              PULLING OUT . . .
```

Dressed in a truly massive and spectacular frock, FELICIA is on top of 'Priscilla,' sitting in a giant silver shoe. The enormous twelve-foot tails on her garment are twirling lyrically in the burning breeze. It is a sight to behold.[4]

In this example, the moment is purely visual, yet Elliott utilized very minimal camera direction.

The only exception to this practice is when you're directing and writing your own scripts. Keep in mind, however, that actors will still need to read the script and you may be less likely to attract great talent if readers have to wade through loads of camera direction.

Different formats exist for different media. Television scripts are more tightly structured than most feature film scripts since commercial television stories must be told within a rigid timeframe, allowing for commercial interruptions. If you are interested in writing for television, the best guidelines are found in scripts of existing series and recent miniseries or **movies-of-the-week**, more commonly referred to as **M.O.W.** Though some of the conventions for script format pertain to television as well as to film, the suggestions provided herein specifically address feature-length films intended for theatrical, cable television, or straight-to-video distribution.

The expected length for a feature-length script is 90 to 120 pages. One script page equals approximately a minute of screen time. This differs somewhat in animation since animation scripts usually include far more action and descriptive language. Unlike the writers of live action scripts, animation writers are encouraged to provide direction within the script.

The following sample scene should help you further understand scriptwriting conventions. The words in *italics* on the right identify the respective elements of the script. Read this scene and jot down what you notice about the format.

FADE IN: ***Transition***

INT. BEDROOM - MORNING   ***Slugline***

PATRICIA MANNING, a bleary-eyed scriptwriter,   **Action**
hunches over her battered computer, oblivious to the
unmade bed, precariously stacked books, and dirty cups
cluttering the tiny room. In her forties, she's still
a looker though her the-hell-with-it attitude under-
mines any edge she might have on beauty.

The phone RINGS. Patricia searches for the origin of
the sound. As the phone continues RINGING, Patricia
talks to no one in particular.

PATRICIA	*Character*
Probably another bill collector lusting after me.	*Dialogue*

The answering machine kicks in. *Action*

PATRICIA'S MACHINE (V.O.)	*Character*
I'm obviously not available so call back later unless . . .	*Dialogue*

Patricia finds the phone beneath a pile *Action*
of tattered *Hollywood Reporters* and snatches
it up.

PATRICIA	*Character*
Yeah.	*Dialogue*

It's her agent and first cousin, MURRAY. *Action*

MURRAY (V. O.)	*Character*
(annoyed)	*Parenthetical*
How many times I gotta tell you not to answer the phone like that? And what's with the message on the machine? I told you, make it nice, you know, classy, like: "You've reached the residence of Patricia . . ."	*Dialogue*

PATRICIA	*Character*
(interrupting)	*Parenthetical*
I appreciate your professional support and encouragement.	*Dialogue*
(beat)	*Parenthetical*
What d'ya want, Murray?	*Dialogue*

MURRAY (V. O.)	*Character*
Any other out-of-work scriptwriter would be begging to hear from his agent . . .	*Dialogue*

PATRICIA	*Character*
Her.	*Dialogue*

```
            MURRAY (V. O.)              Character
        Her? What're ya talking        Dialogue
        her?

            PATRICIA                    Character
        Her agent. You said            Dialogue
        "his agent."

            MURRAY (V. O.)              Character
        That's it. Call me when        Dialogue
        you get serious.
```

Patricia hears Murray SLAM the receiver down. **Action**

CUT TO: ***Transition***

Although Patricia may be a lively character, her behavior is hardly professional. As you read through the script, were you able to identify the elements of the script? Can you distinguish one element from another?

Now that you've seen the elements in context, the glossary that follows should reinforce your understanding of the script elements. Keep in mind that these are generally accepted conventions of the medium. Even produced scripts vary in their execution. Some writers adhere more closely to convention than others. However, it's important to know what conventions are expected of professional scriptwriters. The terms below are presented in the order in which they appear in the sample script.

Transition: A transition specifies a shift in time, place, and/or action. At one time, transitions were used after every scene, but format conventions have changed, and transitions are now used more sparingly, primarily when there's a *dramatic* change. Written entirely in capital letters immediately followed by a colon, transitions should be flush with the left or right margin, either seems to be acceptable. Frequently used transitions include: FADE IN:, FADE OUT:, CUT TO:, DISSOLVE TO:, MATCH CUT:, SMASH CUT:, FLASHFORWARD TO:, or FLASHBACK TO:.

Slugline: A slugline reveals where and when a scene is taking place. The entire slugline should be written in capital letters. The first part of the slugline tells the reader whether the scene is occurring outside or inside. An outside shot is designated as exterior and is represented by the abbreviation EXT.; an inside shot signifies an interior shot and is abbreviated INT. The second part of a slugline, which is separated from the first part by a space, indicates the specific location of the scene. The last part, which is separated from the second by a space-dash-space, tells when the scene occurs. Though you could specify any time of day or night, it's best to generalize as day or night unless a specific time is germane to the story. During production, it often takes a very long time to set up and get a shot. If the time is short-lived, as at sunset, it's difficult to get the shot and also

to match shots in postproduction. If a series of scenes occur within the same time frame, it's not necessary to keep specifying day or night.

Action: Action tells the reader what is happening in the scene and is expressed through descriptive language written in traditional prose style, although the first time a character is introduced the character's name should be capitalized. Often sounds are also capitalized, though that practice seems to be waning. Extended action sequences should be broken into paragraphs separated by a line in block paragraph style. Action should create the mood and describe what's happening, using language economically. You should also write in the present tense to create a sense of immediacy. Whenever possible, use active rather than passive verbs to describe action. Though some writers like to tell the story from the first person plural, some readers are put off by the overuse of "we." If you want to play it safe, avoid using the first person plural.

Character: This signifies which character is speaking within the dialogue. Character is written in capital letters, centered on the page, immediately preceding that character's dialogue. A character need not be human—a character could be an animal, alien, machine, etc. Even if the character isn't present, the character's voice may be heard. You may have noticed the letters V.O. or O.S. in parentheses following the character's name on the same line. These stand for voice-over and off-screen, respectively. Voice-over is generally used as a means of conveying the character's thoughts when the character is visible but not speaking aloud or when the character's voice is heard on a phone or answering machine. Off-screen usually conveys the character's words or ideas when the character isn't visible on screen. Another term which is used to imply that the audience is hearing the character's thoughts is ON TRACK, a term that alludes to the process of imposing the lines on the soundtrack in postproduction. It's up to you to decide which of these terms is most appropriate in any given circumstance.

Dialogue: Dialogue represents the words expressed by your characters. Dialogue is indented, immediately follows the name of the character who is uttering the dialogue, and is written in traditional prose.

Parenthetical expression: Parenthetical expression functions as an aside to the reader to specify the expression of the character who's delivering the line. Parenthetical expression is indented, framed in parentheses, and placed between the character and the dialogue or interjected between lines of dialogue. Use parenthetical expression sparingly. Just as directors don't want excessive camera direction, actors don't want excessive parenthetical expression. Sometimes parenthetical expression indicates a pause in the dialogue. When this happens, the word "beat" is used in place of "pause" and is placed, in parentheses, on its own line separating the dialogue that precedes and follows it.

Familiarizing yourself with these terms not only expands your professional vocabulary, it also provides essential knowledge if you plan to use any scriptwriting software. In some programs, scriptwriting software requires that you "tell" the computer what element you're formatting,

making it necessary for you to know the terminology in order to utilize the software.

Scriptwriting software is invaluable. Once you've mastered a program, you'll be able to concentrate on the substance of your story rather than the distractions of formatting. Most of today's software is so user-friendly that you'll be able to learn the software within an hour.

Should you shop for software, try to find a program that is compatible with your individual needs and existing hardware. Most software programs are available for use with either a Mac or PC. Be sure to read all the specifications on the package to determine what hardware is needed *before* you purchase the software. Most manufacturers also have brochures that highlight the features of the programs so you can compare and contrast programs. You can also check out manufacturers' web sites to sample their wares. Before you decide on the software that's right for you, you may want to ask yourself some of these questions:

- Is the program compatible with your hardware?
- Does your hardware have enough memory to support the program?
- Is it a stand-alone program; that is, can the software function independently or must it interface with another software program in order to operate?
- How do the features of this software compare with those of other types of scriptwriting software?
- What kind of flexibility and features does the program need to have to meet your needs?
- Is the program capable of formatting scripts for radio, television, video, or multilinear stories? Will the program also format plays?
- What kind of warranties and guarantees come with the product?
- Does the manufacturer provide upgrades for the program? If so, are they included in the purchase price or will they be an additional expense?
- Does the manufacturer provide a 1–800 help line to answer your questions? If so, during what hours is help available?
- How does the price of the software compare with the price of comparable programs?
- Is the manufacturer willing to negotiate on the price or are student, senior citizen, or educational discounts available?

Of course, it makes sense to ask other writers what they might recommend, but keep in mind that they may have built-in biases. I've seen perfectly rational people get into ridiculous arguments over the superiority of one system or software over another. Identify your specific needs and let those needs be the deciding factor.

One of the joys of scriptwriting software is the professional appearance of the finished script. You won't need to worry about measuring margins since the software does all that (and much more) for you.

Your finished script should be typed in standard script format, submitted on three-hole punched, 8-1/2" × 11" white bond paper, and covered by two sheets of three-hole punched, neutral-colored card stock. Bind the pages with metal brads (brass paper fasteners sold in boxes at office supply stores), making sure the head is large enough to keep the pages from shifting or slipping through. You may also choose to use washers to hold the brads in place, though they certainly aren't necessary. Also, make sure you include a cover page that provides the name of the script as well as your name and address. If your script is copyrighted, that should also be indicated on the cover page.

If you've read any existing scripts, you may have noticed some numbers in the margins. These numbers identify scenes and are only found in **shooting scripts**, the scripts used in the actual production of the film. Numbering scenes is valuable for scheduling and budgeting a script but numbered scenes don't belong in a script you might send to an agent or producer. Keep your script as clean and unobstructed as possible. The goal is to keep the reader engaged in the story rather than distracted by production concerns.

Now that you know the conventions, don't let them overwhelm you. You'll master them in time. It's far more important that you concentrate on the substance of your story. Everything else will follow.

REFERENCES

1. Hal Hartley, *Henry Fool*, True Fiction Pictures/The Shooting Gallery, 1997.
2. James Charlton and Lisbeth Mark, *The Writer's Home Companion*, Penguin Books, New York, 1987, p. 115.
3. Ray Bradbury, *Zen in the Art of Writing*, Bantam Books, New York, 1990, pp. 39–40.
4. Stephan Elliott, *The Adventures of Priscilla Queen of the Desert*, Currency Press, Sydney, 1994, p. 26.

6

Shaping Stories

This story's gonna grab people! It's about this guy, he's crazy about this girl, but he likes to wear dresses. Should he tell her? Should he not tell her!? He's torn, Georgie! This is drama!

> —Edward D. Wood, Jr. (Johnny Depp) from *Ed Wood*[1]

Scriptwriters are visual storytellers. Like every good storyteller, a scriptwriter shapes the thoughts and stirs the emotions of the audience. In this context, the scriptwriter becomes a contemporary Shaper, so christened by John Gardner in his novel, *Grendel.*

The novel, a retelling of the epic poem "Beowulf" told from the monster's point of view, evokes a medieval past when storytellers shaped the collective consciousness of the populace. As the monster Grendel perches in a tree outside the meadhall, his thoughts are of the Shaper.

> So he sang—or intoned, with the harp behind him, twisting together like sailors' ropes the bits and pieces of the best old songs. The people were hushed. Even the surrounding hills were hushed, as if brought low by language. He knew his art. He was the king of the Shapers, harpstring scratchers (oakmoss-bearded, inspired by winds) . . . What was he? The man had changed the world, had torn up the past by its thick, gnarled roots and had transmuted it, and they, who knew the truth, remembered it his way—and so did I.[2]

The Shaper understands the power of story and how to harness it. In order to become a Shaper in your own right, you need to tell a good story.

A good story is as necessary as the first crocus pushing through the hardened, spent soil of winter. Take a few minutes to think about stories.

105

How do you define story? What do all stories have in common? Can stories be symbolic? Should stories have morals? Do all good stories share the same elements?

How have stories played a role in your life? What are your earliest memories of stories? Close your eyes and think of yourself as a child again. Remember when you were so small that you had to sit on the phonebook to reach the table to eat? Maybe you even had those footed pajamas. Try to remember when your hands were so little that you had trouble tying your shoes. Now think of the stories you heard when you were a child. Did any of the stories disturb you? Anyone who's read the Grimm brothers' fairy tales, or, more recently, Maurice Sendak's, has experienced the dark side of a tale. What stories made you giggle? Which stories from childhood remain in your memory? Does your family tell stories about family members? What stories would you tell your children about your family? What stories about your family would you never tell your children? Are there stories to which you return again and again? If so, how does the story continue to draw you back? Think about your favorite films. What are they? Is it the story, the visual, or the synthesis of both that engages you? Write a list of your favorite stories. Can you identify any elements common to all of the stories?

What, if anything, did you discover about story from your list? Were there elements common to all the stories you listed?

In its simplest terms, a story is a narrating or relating of events or a sequence of events that may be true or fictitious. A story has a beginning, middle, and end, and is populated by human, creature, mechanical, technological, or spiritual characters whose fates the audience comes to care about. Those characters who inhabit a story often have obstacles to overcome, and much of the story may be devoted to the conflicts characters encounter as they try to solve their problems.

Conflicts come in many configurations. A character may have an internal conflict, or the conflict could be with another character or characters, with the natural world, or with society. Although in your life you might wish you could avoid problems, a story would be deadly dull without conflict.

What constitutes a good story? The answer may differ greatly from person to person. For many people, a good story is an action-packed, hair-raising adventure. For others, a good story is about memorable characters who help us reflect upon our own humanity. Yet others enjoy any story that makes them laugh aloud and escape their everyday problems. The history

and mood of the viewer determine the reception of the story. Aren't there days, for instance, when you're not in the mood for a dark story even though you're generally drawn to such stories?

What this variety of needs tells us about story is that there is a longing for different kinds of stories at different times in our lives. My friend and mentor, Cindy Fidler, says that stories are analogous to bananas and artichokes. A banana is readily available, easily peeled, sweet to the taste, and quickly devoured, digested, and forgotten. An artichoke is difficult to find and requires an acquired taste, careful preparation, and great patience. As you peel away the artichoke's multi-layered leaves, your taste is refined, preparing itself for the sweetness of the heart. Once you've savored the heart, you're left with a long-lasting, deep satisfaction. Humans need both banana and artichoke stories. As a scriptwriter, you need to decide which of these stories you dare to tell.

When you begin shaping your story, you will need to carefully construct the world in which your characters reside. It doesn't matter what kind of logic you utilize when you create your story world, as long as the logic you employ is consistent. If your story occurs during the fifteenth century, you should accurately represent the world through the physical environment as well as the characters' collective behavior. In this world, a character in a space suit would be incongruent, unless that character is a time-traveler from another period. Even if you consciously break the rules of logic for comic effect, you still must have established clear rules before you break them.

Once you've created your world, you need to entice the audience to enter that world. A good story immediately grabs an audience's attention, making them hunger for more. In the first ten pages of any script, you should establish the tone of the story, when and where the story is taking place, and to whom it is occurring. It is also extremely important that you create enough curiosity to hook the audience. Drawing an audience into a story is a form of seduction—and seduction involves a gradual revealing. In his book *Zen and the Art of Screenwriting*, William Froug discusses the importance of withholding information and the art of when to reveal.

> In the world of screenwriting, this [curiosity] is called creating *the need to know*. Along with surprise, the need to know is one of the most important tools the storyteller must use to hold his or her audience . . . Avoid telling your audience everything. Withheld information is worth its weight in rubies.[3]

Hooking the reader immediately and utilizing revealing as a form of enticement are essential techniques for the scriptwriter. When you submit a script to an agent, producer, or studio, it will first be read by a professional **reader**. Readers provide **coverage**, a written evaluation of the

script, including a synopsis and commentary. Readers often make judgments about your writing skills and the power of your story within the first ten pages of your script. If you haven't captured the reader's interest by then, if you haven't yet created "the need to know," the reader may lose interest before reaching the marrow of your story.

VISUAL THINKING

While you write your script, you need to think visually. Before you write a scene, close your eyes and imagine the scene in your mind. Can you see the place, the characters, the action? You need to be able to briefly and succinctly describe what you see. Don't write down every detail, just suggest the scene. The classic maxim to remember is **SHOW DON'T TELL**.

Your challenge to tell a good story as a scriptwriter differs from that of a fiction writer or poet. Poets and writers of prose must invite the reader to envision places and people abstracted from language. Since the language of filmmaking utilizes concrete images to tell a story, scriptwriters rely on visual rather than lexical imagery. A novelist, for instance, might create an autumnal scene by writing lengthy passages describing the hues of the oak leaves, the slate-gray sky, and the crispness in the air. For the scriptwriter, it's sufficient to say it's autumn; long passages of descriptive language are unnecessary. Since small visual details often subtly provide information necessary to the viewer, the cold might be suggested through the action as steamy vapors emanating from the characters' mouths. The trick is to give a strong sense of the place and characters, leaving enough room for the reader to imagine the story and the director to manifest the vision.

Alan Ball, writer of the critically acclaimed, award-winning *American Beauty* (Golden Globe and Oscar for Best Original Screenplay), powerfully suggests visual details without dictating direction. Ball's main character, Lester (Kevin Spacey), a despondent, frustrated middle-aged man, experiences a reawakening in the story. An explosion of sensations that he has long denied himself erupts within him when he sees his daughter's friend, Angela (Mena Suvari), on the basketball court. Ball effectively conveys Lester's point of view as Lester fantasizes about Angela.

> Angela looks directly at us now, dancing only for Lester. Her movements take on a blatantly erotic edge as she starts to unzip her uniform, teasing us with an expression that's both innocent and knowing, then . . . she pulls her uniform OPEN and a profusion of RED ROSE PETALS spill forth . . .[4]

Ball relies primarily on visual details to spin out the lush, dreamy sequences and sustain the visual themes. Thematically, the color red runs

through the story like a pulsating artery, infusing the script with a powerful visual subtext. Stolen from the red of the American Beauty rose, the color saturates the story visually and figuratively. Reading beyond the satiny surface of the rose petals, the red represents fleeting beauty, awakened passion, blossoming youth, sexual awakening, and, ultimately, death as spiritual transformation.

If you have difficulty thinking visually, try to write your story first as a silent film. Keep it short; a page or two will do. If you find you can't tell the story without the dialogue, then your story may not be able to be told visually, or perhaps you simply need to re-imagine your story. Another tactic is to imagine yourself in a blackened theatre. What is the first image the audience will see? Where is the story happening and to whom? What happens after the credits roll?

If you're still having trouble imagining the visuals, it may be helpful to read comic books and children's picture books. These venues use many cinematic conventions to relay the story visually and introduce you to basic composition within and between frames or pages.

Good films create the illusion that everything is happening in fluid motion. In reality, films are a compilation of shots edited together to make a conceptual whole. If you can begin to think in shots, it may help you to conceptualize your story visually.

Purposeful shots can convey point of view, stasis or energy, isolation or intimacy, power or vulnerability, and the passing of time. Cinematic time is very different from "real" time since it can be compressed or expanded. Shots may have theoretical relationships to one another as well. Though a series of shots is often described as a **montage**, the tradition of montage in film is to juxtapose shots (often ironically) to create a whole that's conceptually greater than the sum of its parts. Studying film history and aesthetics will enhance your understanding of the conceptual relationship between narrative elements and visual style.

Familiarizing yourself with some of the basic camera shots and movements used in composing images may help you "see" the film in your mind. This information will be especially helpful if you would like to direct your film as well as write it. If you don't plan to direct, it may be helpful for you to imagine the film as a series of images that visually embody your story.

Here are some of the basic camera shots and movements.

ESTABLISHING SHOT (EST): A shot, usually a long shot, that establishes the location of the story's setting and may help establish the mood or tone of the work.

MASTER SHOT: A shot that establishes the environment and everyone in that environment.

LONG SHOT (LS): A shot taken from a long distance that fully reveals the subject and the surrounding environment.

MEDIUM SHOT (MS): A shot taken at a middle distance from the subject. A medium shot reveals part of an object or a person (usually from the waist up on a person).

CLOSE UP (CU): A close up focuses tightly on a specific object or person (usually from the shoulders up on a person). In *Fight Club*, a close up of Marla (Helena Bonham Carter), partially hidden beneath a hat, frames her as the object of desire and perpetuates the mysterious nature of her character.

EXTREME CLOSE UP (ECU): A very close shot of a specific detail or portion of a person such as the eyes. In *Citizen Kane*, when Kane (Orson Welles) whispers "Rosebud" in ECU, the shot foreshadows the ending of the film.

POINT OF VIEW (POV): A shot from a camera position that is aligned with a character's line of sight so that the audience identifies with the character's point of view. Hitchcock used this shot extensively in *Rear Window* when the audience views much of the action through the main character's, L. B. Jeffries's (James Stewart), point of view.

LOW ANGLE: The position of the camera points upward at an extreme angle, placing the viewer at a psychologically inferior position while making the subject appear dominant or forbidding. This is also a good angle for establishing point of view. The film *Witches* uses a lot of low angle shots to help the viewer identify with the story from the boys' points of view once they've been turned into mice.

HIGH ANGLE: The position of the camera points downward at an extreme angle in a position above the action, placing the viewer at a psychologically superior point of view while making the subject appear inferior or ordinary. Hitchcock used a number of high angle shots to help the viewer identify with Scottie's (James Stewart) fear of heights in *Vertigo*.

OVERHEAD SHOT: A shot positioned directly above the subject. In Zhang Yimou's *Raise the Red Lantern*, an overhead shot of the Master's house depicts a series of boxed-in courtyards, exemplifying the trapped feelings of the young, isolated Fourth Wife, Songlian (Gong Li).

AERIAL SHOT: A shot taken from an aircraft positioned far above the subject. This shot is often used to create a godlike or heavenly perspective. Wim Wenders used a number of aerial shots to establish the point of view of the angel, Damiel (Bruno Ganz), in *Wings of Desire*.

PAN: A smooth-moving shot produced by a mounted camera that moves to the right or left along a horizontal plane, sometimes following a subject.

DOLLY: A smooth-moving shot produced by a camera mounted on a wheeled platform or track. Moving into the scene is considered a DOLLY IN; moving out of a scene is a DOLLY OUT.

TRACKING SHOT: A camera movement in which the camera body moves through space in a horizontal path. On the screen, it produces a mobile framing that travels through space forward, backward, or to one side. The opening tracking shot of Paul Thomas Anderson's *Boogie Nights* creates an organic feel for the subculture it depicts while introducing the characters. The shot also replicates one used in *Goodfellas* as a visual homage to director Martin Scorsese.

These camera shots and movements are by no means all inclusive. They are included primarily to help you think visually and also to help you understand the jargon of the profession. As mentioned earlier, you really shouldn't include specific camera direction within your script unless it's absolutely essential to your story or unless you're sure you'll be directing the story. Your script should awaken imaginative longings within the reader rather than dull the senses with excessive camera direction.

DESPERATELY SEEKING STRUCTURE

Rarely does a writer simply sit down and start writing a script without an organized structure in mind. Getting the structure from the mind to the page is less intimidating if you know how to structure each scene.

A scene is an event, action, or interaction having unity of time and place. The structure of your story is composed through the sequencing, or ordering, of your scenes. Scenes may be ordered according to logic, chronology, space, cause and effect, or a combination of these elements.

Each scene should exist to propel the story forward. Though each scene should have a beginning, middle, and end and be complete unto itself, it's also important that the relationship between scenes be carefully constructed. Just as synergism creates an effect greater than the sum of its respective elements, so should scenes create a dynamic that enhances the story. Tension within and between scenes is also crucial to the thrust of the story. Without tension, the audience loses its involvement and concern for the characters.

If you think of your script as a dynamic whole, the scenes are the components that comprise the whole. Though you may have slept through your high school physics class, physics definitely influence your story. Just as nuclear energy is created from the collision of atoms, your story derives energy and momentum from the collision of scenes. As you stack scenes up against one another, some will congeal, some collide, some ignite, some explode, and some dissipate. It's the relationship of scenes to one another that creates energy and tension in your story. Just as a physicist experiments with the dynamics of physical elements, a scriptwriter experiments with the dynamics of story elements.

One of the most challenging aspects of scriptwriting is determining how to arrange scenes and deciding which scenes are absolutely necessary to the whole story. In order to answer this challenge, you need to know the purpose of each individual scene. Every scene should reveal where and when the action is occurring, who is involved, and why the action is occurring. In the overall structure of the story, scenes should build "the need to know," drive the momentum of the story, and reveal an understanding of the characters and their respective motivations. One of the most painful

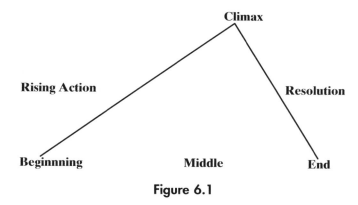

Figure 6.1

decisions you may have to make is to eliminate a scene you love if it serves
no purpose in the development of the story.

Scenes don't exist in some narrative existential space. Without structure, scenes are only scenes. As you begin to shape your ideas into script
form, you'll need to start conceptualizing the structure of your story. Structure is the framework or skeleton that gives definition and support to your
scenes. A successfully structured story will create a dynamic among the
interdependent scenes to propel the story forward.

Classic dramatic structure is represented in a paradigm that looks like
a mountain, as shown in Figure 6.1. The structure includes a beginning,
middle, and end. The beginning marks the lowest point on the paradigm
and the start of the rising action. At this point, the story should be set up.
Rising action infers a building of action and dramatic tension, comprising
the middle portion of the story. Obstacles will occur in this part of the
story. The action continues to rise until the climax, the most intense
point of excitement. The climax is followed by the resolution, which ends
the story.

In many ways, finding a structure for your story is much like mountain
climbing. You must start with your feet on the ground, then begin your
arduous ascent, struggling with any obstacles you encumber on the path.
As you climb the mountain, you will sometimes fall into deep crevices and
lose sight of the summit. You must remain undeterred until you finally
reach the pinnacle, where you will find a profound sense of satisfaction and
accomplishment. The energy you expend to climb the mountain is similar
to the energy you'll find in a tightly structured script.

One of the most widely applied structural paradigms is that of a teacher
and writer named Syd Field. A fairly rigid paradigm, Field's structure
divides a story into three distinct acts. In the first act, from page 1–30, the
story is set up, and a plot point is introduced between pages 25–27.
Field defines a plot point as "an incident, episode, or event that 'hooks'

into the action and spins it around into another direction."[5] In the second act, from pages 30–90, a confrontation occurs, followed by a second plot point on pages 85–90. In the third act, from pages 90–120, the story is resolved.

An exemplary use of this paradigm is found in Robert Towne's script *Chinatown*. Towne's skillfully crafted story invites the viewer to participate in the unraveling of a mystery. Jake Gittes (Jack Nicholson), a private detective, is hired by the alleged Mrs. Evelyn Mulwray (Diane Ladd) to find out if her husband is cheating on her. As Jake begins what he believes is a routine investigation, he is drawn into a tale of political corruption and dark family secrets that eventually lead him to Chinatown, a place that forces Jake to confront his own dark past. *Chinatown* follows a three-act structure with two plot points. The first occurs when the real Mrs. Mulwray (Faye Dunaway) appears in Jake's office. The second appears when Jake discovers that the glasses found in the pond previously assumed to be those of Evelyn's dead husband are bifocals, implicating Evelyn Mulwray's father, Noah (John Huston), in the death of her husband.[6]

Though there is certainly much to be garnered from Field's paradigm, it's important to recognize that this structure is the successor of the dramatic play, a form designed for live theatre. When you attend a play, each act has a specific purpose, and the end of the act signifies a time to pause and reflect. This form resembles commercial television, since the narrative is formulated to be viewed in acts. Theatrical films as well as some cable films are intended to be a sustained viewing experience. One of the goals of the story should be to engage the audience without interruption. Thinking in acts may not always be the best method for structuring a script intended for film viewing.

In an interview with Oliver Stone, George Hickenlooper asked the question, "Do you think there's new ground to be broken with respect to the film narrative as a visual medium rather than as a three-act play in the Aristotelian sense?"

Stone responded:

> I think that's what keeps a lot of people going. There's that feeling that we're in the first century of development of a new form, like in medicine. There're new avenues to explore all the time. But ultimately there are classical truths that seem to come to bear which go back to the *Odyssey* and *Iliad*, through Dante, Shakespeare and Dickens. I mean, there are certain things that interest people. I think people identify with other people. You can't quite get away from that.[7]

In *The Writer's Journey: Mythic Structure for Storytellers and Screenwriters*, Christopher Vogler, story consultant and 20th Century Fox executive, reveals how classic structure supports the universal truths to which Stone alludes. Vogler has devised a paradigm, influenced by Joseph Camp-

bell's *The Hero of a Thousand Faces*, that parallels the hero's journey. In act one of Vogler's paradigm, the hero leaves the ordinary world when called to adventure. Once on the journey, the hero refuses the call, then meets a mentor who helps the hero over the first threshold. Crossing the threshold marks the foray into the second act, where the hero encounters tests, allies, and enemies; approaches the inmost cave; endures the supreme ordeal; and takes possession of the reward. Once the reward is in hand, the third act ensues as the hero takes the road back to the ordinary world, experiences a resurrection, and brings back an elixir.

Vogler emphasizes the need to see the hero's journey as a flexible paradigm.

> The Hero's Journey is a skeletal framework that should be fleshed out with the details and surprises of the individual story. The structure should not call attention to itself, nor should it be followed too precisely. The order of the stages given here is only one of many possible variations. The stages can be deleted, added to, and drastically shuffled without losing any of their power.[8]

To fully appreciate the hero's journey and the heroes, mentors, guardians, heralds, shapeshifters, shadows, and tricksters who inhabit the pages of Vogler's book, you would be better served to read the work in its entirety. It's an especially significant work for anyone who is not well read for it introduces a rich landscape of literary allusion.

Andrew Horton presents other possibilities for narrative structures in his book, *Writing the Character-Centered Screenplay*. He introduces the following paradigms:

- the "circular tale," a story that ends where it began;
- the "tale within a tale," a framing "narrative within which the main tale exists;"
- a "multiple point of view narrative" that tells the story from varying points of view; and
- the "collage narrative" that weaves eclectic narrative styles together into the whole fabric of the film.[9]

Horton's book illuminates the necessity of thinking beyond the confines of traditional paradigms.

Two other paradigms you may consider are what might be termed interwoven and convergent narratives. **Interwoven narrative** presents multiple storylines that may overlap or intersect throughout the story to create a dynamic among the respective storylines and support a thematic link between them. The storylines may be intertwined through time, character, place, or any configuration of these elements. *Nashville*, written by

Joan Tewkesbury, and *Short Cuts*, written by Frank Barhydt and director Robert Altman, are exemplary films employing interwoven narrative. **Convergent narrative** utilizes a similar structure. In this paradigm, several different storylines that appear to have no relationship to one another in the development of the story converge at the end of the story, resolving the story and revealing the relationships between the respective storylines. *Playing by Heart*, written by Willard Carroll, and *200 Cigarettes*, written by Shana Larsen, employ this structure.

Any paradigm should provide a framework for thought from which you'll be able to shape your story. Ultimately, the structure should arise from the needs of the story rather than from any particular paradigm. Structure shouldn't be imposed upon the story from forces outside the story but should come from within, supporting the conceptual spine of the story. If a structure doesn't exist to satisfy your needs, you may want to experiment with less conventional structures or create a hybrid structure of your own.

An excellent example of a script that doesn't employ conventional structure is Patricia Lousianna Knop's *Siesta*. The main character, Claire (Ellen Barkin), finds herself lying bloodied, disheveled, and confused on an airfield in Spain. As the story progresses, Claire pieces her history together in a series of flashbacks that we assume are digressing from the present. In a jumbled sequence of scenes, Claire moves in and out of the past and present, in and out of her present life as a daredevil skydiver in Texas with her husband, Del (Martin Sheen), and her former life as an acrobat in Spain with her lover, Augustine (Gabriel Byrne). The viewer, like Claire, is actively engaged in reconstructing the events of Claire's life to make some sense of the narrative. By the end of the story, the means have justified the end (which I won't reveal in case you haven't seen the film). The nonlinear structure of the story heightens the viewer's curiosity and conceptually manifests Claire's confusion as her mind attempts to piece together fragments of memory and experience.[10] Had the film been structured according to a traditional, chronologically developed paradigm, the story would have lacked energy and "the need to know." The nonlinear structure draws the reader into the story, stimulates the imagination, and heightens the story's tension as the action progresses.

Nonlinear structure is difficult to define since linear films may use flashbacks within the linear storyline and nonlinear films often utilize linear sequences within the overall story. The difference resides in the way in which the structure unifies the theme of the story as well as in the purpose that the writer has in mind when developing the story. The purpose may be to express differing points of view. In the classic film, *Rashomon*, writer-director Akira Kurosawa depicts the same crime from four distinctly different points of view. In each narrative sequence, the rape victim, the murdered husband, the marauding bandit, and the bystander, respectively,

tell their stories. Since each sequence is thoughtfully developed and juxta-posed, the fragmented parts of the narrative are understood as a whole. By utilizing disparate points of view, Kurosawa emphasizes the subjectivity of truth and the fragility of justice.

Quentin Tarantino's scripts also rely heavily on nonlinear narrative. He cites the novel as his influence.

> When you read a book the writer thinks nothing of starting in the middle of the story. In chapter four or something it goes into a character's child-hood for a while. Is that a flashback? No, it's just the way the narrator is telling the story. I like using that structure and applying it to film. Not just for the sake of doing it. If the film would have been more dramati-cally engaging by telling it in a beginning-middle-end situation, I would have done that. I actually think the kinda 'answers first, questions later' structure has made it better, made it more involving.[11]

Vogler places Tarantino's nonlinear storytelling in a larger, cultural context, especially with respect to *Pulp Fiction*.

> *Pulp Fiction* reflects the postmodern condition in both style and content. Postmodernism is most apparent in its unusual structure, which disre-gards the conventional cinema's respect for linear time. The sequences appear to have been sliced up with a samurai sword and thrown in the air, although in fact the order of scenes has been carefully chosen to develop a coherent theme and produce a definite emotional effect.[12]

The recent proliferation of the nonlinear structure is indeed the product of a cultural revolution largely influenced by advancements in technology. Computers are shifting the paradigm. As Janet Murray observes in *Hamlet on the Holodeck*, "The existence of hypertext has given writers a new means of experimenting with segmentation, juxtaposition, and connectedness."[13]

A film that exemplifies Murray's assertion is *Run, Lola, Run*. Writer-director Tom Tykwer's frenetically paced structure spins out three possi-ble narratives as his main character, Lola (Franka Potente) tries to save her lover, Manni (Moritz Bleibtreu). In a race against the clock, Lola must get 100,000 marks to save Manni from his gangster boss. Using elements of what Horton calls "collage narrative," combined with a nonlinear narra-tive, Tykwer's inventive story seamlessly utilizes film, video, music, graph-ics, live action, and animation to energize Lola's quest. The fragmented narrative, repeated in three slightly altered sequences, questions the random nature of life. Lola's literal collision with various characters (whose lives are fast-forwarded at breakneck speed) suggests that all of our actions have consequences and that our connections, though seemingly inconse-quential, have meaning.

So how should you structure your script? You may feel a need to rely on an existing paradigm to provide structure, or you may want to experiment with various structures to decide which structure best supports the needs of your story. Only you can discover what works best for you.

Write out three key scenes for a script you're developing. Now place the scenes in chronological order. What needs to happen between these scenes? What comes before and/or after these scenes? Now try arranging these same three scenes in a different order. Think of memory as a framing device. What if your narrator or main character had a memory lapse? How might the order of the scenes change? Now think of your scenes occurring from a completely different point of view. Would the order change? What else might change? Now consider how the scenes would change if each one occurred during a different time period. Would it be possible given the context of your scenes? If so, how might that affect the order of your scenes?

STEPS TO STRUCTURING

Before you begin writing each scene, you should explore the methods other writers have used to flesh out and order scenes. You may have to try several of these methods or devise your own hybrid method until you're satisfied with a technique that works for you.

You may find simple note-taking to be a method that works for you. Some writers I know fill pages of notebooks with copious notes until they have worked out the story to their satisfaction. The advantage of this technique is that once you sit down to write your story, you have a sound foundation from which to work.

If you're an especially vivid visual thinker and the whole story is already in your head, you might try creating a **storyboard**. A storyboard is a pictorial representation of each shot. It looks like a cartoon strip with each shot comprising a single frame. Storyboards may be comprised of primitive sketches or elaborate drawings or paintings. The quality of the picture isn't important. As long as you can interpret what's in each shot, you can create a mental picture of the sequence of the action. It's very labor intensive to storyboard a whole film, and unnecessary, for a screenwriter. Storyboards are often used for complicated action sequences to help choreograph the action. For you, it might be helpful to storyboard a scene to help imagine how it plays out visually.

A **treatment** is another option. Typically, a treatment is comprised of between five to forty-five pages of prose that describe your storyline and

scene sequences with bits of dialogue to liven the narrative. It is not a minute-to-minute account of everything that will happen in your script. A treatment reveals who the main character(s) is/are, what the conflict is, and how the conflict is resolved.

If you have a fairly clear idea of the overall structure in mind, you may want to outline the individual scenes before you begin writing your script. Outlining the scenes is especially helpful since it presents your scenes in a condensed, linear fashion. Chances are your scenes may not remain in that order or that some of the scenes may be eliminated as you write, but it's a good starting place.

A common outline used in the film industry is the step outline, which is comprised of **step sheets**. Step sheets provide the following information for each scene: who is in the scene, where and when the scene takes place, and what happens in the scene.

Another common method of ordering scenes is through the use of **file cards**. File cards may have a number identifying the scene at the top of each card, although some writers prefer not to insert the number until the scenes are properly ordered. Each card will contain the same information included in a step sheet except that it will probably be written in sketchy prose rather than in outline form. Again, that choice belongs to the individual writer. Once the scenes are complete, or as the work progresses, cards may be rearranged in any order as you reconceptualize the structure of your story. If you use scriptwriting software, you may want to choose a program that incorporates a file card feature. Generally, these features enable you to rearrange your cards as well as to insert them as scenes into your script.

If your story has an ensemble cast or one or more subplots, you may find it necessary to graphically plot your varying characters and subplots. It's easy to do this on recycled computer paper (the type with perforated edges and continuously connected sheets) rather than on individual sheets. You can spread the paper out on the floor and begin masterminding your plots.

Anna Hamilton Phelan uses a similar technique.

> I used to use index cards, but now I buy a roll of butcher paper. It's about two feet wide, and it's in a long roll, like a scroll. And I write the story out on that. (Talk about linear!) I'll have a scroll twenty, thirty, forty feet long. And I just wind it around my wall so, as I look up, I can really see the whole movie this way, the whole screenplay.[14]

Whatever method you devise to structure your story is the best method for you. Don't let other writers or scriptwriting gurus tell you their way is the only way. You know what works for you.

It would be misleading to assert that once you have your structure in place, you're ready to develop your characters. All of the elements that

shape a story are intricately related and are often developed simultaneously. Chances are that your characters have led you to the story, and the structure is a means of supporting the cultivation of your characters. The next chapter should assist you in fully developing your characters into dimensional beings.

Have you ever tried to solve a manual puzzle, like a Rubik's cube? Have you ever watched someone else try to solve the same problem? Did that person try the same approaches that you did, or did he or she try other approaches? What about math story problems in school? Do you think you solved those problems in the same way that your classmates did? Each of us has unique ways of solving problems. What's the most difficult problem that you've ever had? Were you able to solve it? If so, how? If not, why do you think you were unable to solve it? Do you think you'll be able to solve it at another time in your life?

REFERENCES

1. Scott Alexander, *Ed Wood*, Touchstone Pictures, 1994.
2. John Gardner, *Grendel*, Ballantine Books, New York, 1971, pp. 35–6.
3. William Froug, *Zen and the Art of Screenwriting: Insights and Interviews*, Silman-James Press, Los Angeles, 1996, p. 21.
4. Alan Ball, *American Beauty*, Newmarket Press, New York, 1999, p. 16.
5. Syd Field, *The Screenwriter's Workbook*, Dell Publishing Company, New York, 1984, p. 30.
6. Robert Towne, *Chinatown*, Paramount, 1974.
7. George Hickenlooper, ed., *Reel Conversations: Candid Interviews with Film's Foremost Directors and Critics*, Carol Publishing Group, New York, 1991, p. 124.
8. Christopher Vogler, *The Writer's Journey: Mythic Structure for Storytellers and Screenwriters*, Michael Wiese Productions, Los Angeles, 1992, p. 30.
9. Andrew Horton, *Writing the Character-Centered Screenplay*, University of California Press, Berkeley, 1994, p. 108–9.
10. Patricia Lousianna Knop, *Siesta* (based on a story by Patrice Chaplin), Lorimar Pictures and Siren Pictures, 1987.
11. Jami Bernard, *Quentin Tarantino: The Man and his Movies*, Harper Perennial, New York, 1995, p. 154.
12. Vogler, p. 277.
13. Janet H. Murray, *Hamlet on the Holodeck: The Future of Narrative in Cyberspace*, The MIT Press, Cambridge, 1999, pp. 55–6.
14. William Froug, ed., *The New Screenwriter Looks at the New Screenwriter*, Silman-James Press, Los Angeles, 1991, p. 33.

7

Creating Characters

Movies invent these ridiculous fake plots that reduce the characters to cardboard. It's the characters that need to move your piece.[1]

—Barry Levinson

Oftentimes, the films that remain vital to you long after you've seen them are those whose characters have remained lodged in your mind. Characters who touch you, move you, jolt you to think, feel, and react, live inside you long after the lights in the theatre come up. Whether it be the gentle, wise Atticus Finch from *To Kill A Mockingbird* or the fiery, spirited Scarlett O'Hara from *Gone with the Wind,* these characters remain with you, become part of your collective filmic memory.

Can you imagine a story without characters? As screenwriting teacher and writer William Froug emphatically states, "Characters are story; the two are inextricably linked."[2] As you develop your story, it's impossible to think about story without thinking about character. Whether you have a story with an ensemble of characters, a buddy story, or a story with a single protagonist surrounded by supporting players, your characters are central to any story's success. If the audience doesn't believe in the existence of a character, isn't frightened or moved by a character, or can't identify with a character, you haven't got a story.

You need to think about the purpose of having each character in the story. Why is the character there? Is it just to take the story from point A to point B, or does the audience have something to learn from this character? Is the character subservient to the plot? Do the character's actions reinforce the theme? How does the character interact with other characters? Is there tension between the characters? Does the character exhibit growth during the story? Can the audience identify with or relate to the character? By knowing this character, will the audience's lives be enriched

135

or disturbed? You need to be able to answer these questions to justify the existence of any character.

Where do characters come from? Are they hatched out of some existential egg? They may come from real people who shaped the history of the world or they may come from the recesses of your past. You may find them in your own longings for a life that you don't dare live but one in which your characters will thrive. Wherever you find them, you'll be amazed at how elusive they can be.

CONCEPTUALIZING CHARACTERS

Characters exist to propel the story forward, to engage the reader or viewer in the story, to create tension within the story, and to provide a literal and figurative voice for the theme. Since film is a visual medium, your characters are enlivened primarily through their actions.

In traditional storytelling, the story evolves around the actions of a central character, or **protagonist**, who has an obstacle to overcome or a goal to reach. The protagonist is a hero who has special strengths that enable him or her to overcome obstacles. The obstacle may be in the form of an opponent, or **antagonist**, who creates an opposing force. The antagonist is often associated with evil and is easily identifiable as a negative force.

Though traditional characters have by no means been banished from storytelling, contemporary characters seem to more closely resemble their human counterparts than their larger-than-life predecessors. Contemporary stories may involve two central characters or an ensemble of characters rather than a single protagonist. The antagonist, too, may be far subtler; the antagonist may even be the dark side of the central character. An interesting example of this is in the script, *Fight Club*, adapted from Chuck Palahniuk's novel. The narrator (Edward Norton), a depressed loner whose primary social interactions occur at various 12-step meetings, meets a charismatic salesperson, Tyler Durden (Brad Pitt), on an airplane. As the story progresses, the narrator is drawn deeper and deeper into Tyler's shadowy, violent world. Because the scriptwriter, Jim Uhls, creates such a convincing distinction between the narrator and Tyler, the revelation that Tyler is the narrator's darker side comes as a startling discovery at the story's conclusion.

Fight Club is also a good example of how the internal life of the character is revealed through the external world. The narrator's upscale dwellings, immaculately furnished with sleekly designed furniture, exemplify the hollow center of his life. His relationship with Marla (Helena Bonham Carter) is equally vacuous. Both are 12-step imposters, "tourists" who share fictions with real victims. Their sexual relationship parallels the

bestial nature of the fights. As the narrator's life begins to unravel, he moves into a boarded-up, abandoned dwelling, one as empty as he is. Only when he confronts his own emptiness and frees himself from the prison of modern life is he able to understand himself within the cultural context of a material, emasculating society.[3]

So how do you reveal the longings, fears, needs, wants, and drives of the character through action? In order to answer that question, you have to be able to define both the interior and exterior dimensions of your character. This is achieved by creating a backstory.

BACKSTORY

Just as humans are the sum of their experiences, characters, too, are the culmination of their experiences. Before you breathe life into your character, you need to think through your character's experiential history. Constructing a history for your character involves creating a backstory.

Consider Carlos. He's a lonely guy until he meets Anna, a vivacious, intelligent woman, on the commuter train. She invites him to her apartment for dinner. Carlos hasn't dated in months, maybe years; it's been so long he can't remember. Though he's apprehensive, he's also excited. He likes Anna's openness and feels comfortable talking to her.

Carlos wants everything to be perfect. He brings Anna a gift—a book of poetry. Anna is touched by his thoughtfulness and the evening is off to a sweet start. As Carlos lights the candles at the intimate dinner table, Anna brings out a rare wine and confesses that she spent a week's wages on it. Suddenly, Carlos's mood shifts. He refuses the wine and grows somber, distant. Carlos decides to leave before he finishes his meal. The night is a disaster. Why?

It's impossible to understand Carlos's behavior without knowing his backstory. Carlos has recently come to terms with the fact that he's an alcoholic. He thought he had his emotions and addiction under control but when Anna brought out the wine and confessed that she had saved her wages for a week to buy it, Carlos came undone. He was ashamed of his alcoholism and unable to tell Anna the truth.

Backstory is essential in order to determine how a character will behave in any given situation. Without a backstory, it's impossible to understand what motivates a character's behavior. Characters do not exist in a void without experiential, environmental, or physiological influences that define who they are or who they may become.

How do you shape a character, create a backstory? Every character has an **exterior** and **interior** life. The exterior life is represented by that which is visible to the viewer; the interior life is that which occurs inside the mind, body, and spirit of the character and is revealed through the use of visual

details and the character's interaction with the environment and with other characters.

The exterior life of the character includes the character's physical and social traits:

Physical
- ethnic/racial distinctions
- planetary, mechanical, imaginative, or creature distinctions
- body (age, sex, height, weight, coloring, sexual appeal, etc.)
- appearance (neat, well-dressed, sloppy, unkempt, etc.)
- verbal dexterity
- physical impairments/physical carriage/metabolism
- idiosyncrasies/habits

Social
- class (lower, middle, upper, marginal)
- environment
- education or lack of it
- income or lack of it
- employment or lack of it
- skills
- friends
- family/family history

The interior life of the character includes the character's intellectual, psychological, and spiritual traits:

Intellectual
- mental capabilities
- imagination/creativity
- philosophical thinking
- ambitions/goals

Psychological
- childhood memories and experiences
- sensitivity toward self and others
- fears/phobias/hang-ups
- failures/disappointments
- sexual attitudes
- socialization skills
- awareness/perception
- outlook on life (optimistic, pessimistic, fatalistic, etc.)

Spiritual
- spiritual beliefs or lack of them
- adherence to organized religious practices
- sensory gifts
- psychic abilities

Keep in mind that the exterior life of the character may conceal as well as reveal the interior life of the character. In fact, they may be in opposition to one another.

In *The Screenplay: A Blend of Film Form and Content*, Margaret Mehring explains the inherent conflict between the inner and outer goals of the character.

> Good characters are simultaneously dealing with an inner, psychological struggle and an outer, physical struggle—an inner goal and an outer goal. The outer goal is the plot goal and the inner goal is a personal goal. These two goals contain conflicting emotions—emotions that cannot both be gratified at the same time. A character can be driven to achieve one goal while being simultaneously compelled to seek a very different and conflicting goal. IT IS THIS WARRING BETWEEN THE EXTERNAL AND INTERNAL GOALS THAT IS THE ESSENCE OF GREAT DRAMA.[4]

Part of your task in creating a character is addressing how you reveal or conceal the inner life of the character within the structure of the story.

While developing your backstory, you might find it helpful to create a mock interview with your character. Write a scene in which your character is being interviewed by one of the following: a psychologist, a best friend, a lover, a reporter from a tabloid television program, a counselor from a dating service, or a potential boss.

Was your character able to answer the questions the interviewer posed? If you're not sure how your character might respond or behave in any given situation, then you might not know all you need to know about your character. How do you find out what you need to know?

You might consider the context in which your character exists. In *Creating Unforgettable Characters*, Linda Seger emphasizes the need for context.

Characters don't exist in a vacuum. They're a product of their environment. A character from seventeenth-century France is different from one from Texas in 1980. A character who practices medicine in a small town in Illinois is different from someone who's the pathologist at Boston General Hospital. Someone who grew up poor on an Iowa farm will be different from one who grew up rich in Charleston, South Carolina. A black, or Hispanic, or Irish-American will be different from a Swede from St. Paul. Understanding a character begins with understanding the context that surrounds the character.[5]

If, for instance, you're writing about someone who has vastly different cultural experiences than you do, you may need to immerse yourself in the roots of the culture. Find out all you can about the language, beliefs, environments, and customs of that culture. If the culture is too removed from your own experience and you feel out of your depth, you may want to abandon that character and give breath and breadth to a character drawn from your own experience or imagination.

Sometimes you create a character whose purpose in the story diminishes as you develop the story. If that's the case, you should consider eliminating the character from the story. Don't despair. Once you've created a character you love, that character will always exist for you. If you want to bring the character to life, hold on to the essence of the character and resurrect that character or a close facsimile in another script.

Though you need to fully understand the backstory of your character in order to determine what drives your character, the audience will only need some of that information. The information should be revealed through visual details and gradual revelation interspersed throughout the dialogue. Avoid telling the audience about the character; show the audience who the character is through his or her environment and interaction with other characters.

Want to test yourself to see if you really know your character? Imagine walking into your character's primary environment. Look in the character's refrigerator. List every item in the refrigerator. Is it easy or difficult to imagine the refrigerator's contents? If it's easy to describe what's in the refrigerator, you probably have a good grasp of your character. If your character doesn't have a refrigerator, or lives in a refrigerator box, how might that information be equally valuable?

In his illuminating article "A Matter of Character," novelist Maynard Allington suggests that creating backstory only addresses the superficial aspects of character.

There is a deeper dimension to personality, and you must search for it in each of your major players. As the casting director of your novel, you should be able to answer the next question: What is the *defining* issue in life that shaped the personality of this character? Know the answer before you ever start to write.[6]

Though Allington's advice is meant for aspiring novelists, his wisdom applies to scriptwriters as well. The source of a defining issue may be a character flaw or a prior experience that altered the direction of your character's life. Once you understand your character's defining issue, you'll be closer to developing a dimensional being.

The notion of a defining issue is best understood by examining the archeology of your own past. Dig around in your memory and dust off some of those experiential artifacts. Is there any single incident or event in your life that has provided a kind of marker, dividing the experiences that came before from those that came after? If so, what was it about that moment that altered the course of your thinking or feeling? Describe yourself as you were before that point in time. Now describe yourself after that point. What essential transformation occurred? Sometimes a defining issue develops slowly over time. Do you ever find yourself repeating patterns in your life, some of which are self-destructive? This could be the result of a flaw in your character created by a defining issue that you haven't identified or addressed. If you can't identify any specific defining issue, think about your adolescence. Almost everyone experiences some kind of shift in thinking, feeling, or behavior during adolescence. You may recall an especially embarrassing or funny incident lingering in your memory. Perhaps your memories of adolescence are more painful. A model screenplay that successfully juxtaposes the comic and painful, sometimes in a single moment, is Todd Solondz's *Welcome to the Dollhouse*. Attempting to identify your own defining issue may bring you closer to understanding the defining issues of your characters.

DIMENSIONAL CHARACTERS

What is a dimensional character? A dimensional character is one who is many-faceted, who has needs, who has weaknesses and flaws as well as strengths, and who may have ambiguous feelings about life or relationships. In other words, a dimensional character is a complex being.

In order to create a complex character, you'll need to identify your character's needs. If your character doesn't need anything, there's nothing to

drive the story forward. You're probably already familiar with basic human needs such as shelter, clothing, food, and water. Characters have even more specific dramatic needs that are identified in Denny Martin Flinn's *How Not to Write a Screenplay*. Flinn cites Robert Ardrey, a playwright and anthropologist, whose theory of the motivation in higher animals asserts that:

> . . . all human beings seek:
>
> Security, Identity and Stimulation
>
> which he defined by their opposites: anxiety, anonymity and boredom. We all seek these three things (assuming human beings can be included in the 'higher animals' category) though not necessarily in equal proportions. While these three 'needs' are not mutually exclusive, Ardrey felt that we are all driven by one or the other as a priority. *Lethal Weapon*'s Martin Riggs is driven by stimulation. *As Good As It Gets* Melvin Udall is driven by security. *Sunset Boulevard*'s Norma Desmond is driven by identity . . . Keep in mind that a character's needs will drive their actions, and their actions will drive your screenplay.[7]

One of the most successfully realized action–driven characters is Indiana Jones. Is he dimensional? Absolutely. He's sometimes indecisive or confused about his emotional state of mind and he has a definite fear of snakes. None of these characteristics fit the mold of the stereotypical hero. His character flaws help make him more vulnerable, and, thus, more likeable. The viewer is able to empathize and identify with him.

Audience identification is important. By identifying with the truths of a character, viewers are able to examine their own truths. Also, if viewers can't relate to or identify with a character, then they may not be able to care about the character.

Character flaws go a long way toward making a character accessible and empathetic and toward creating a fully conceived character. Character flaws are also important since the character needs somewhere to grow. If a character is perfect, or nearly so, there's little opportunity for the character to grow or learn.

Part of the process of identifying with a character is watching the character change as the story progresses. This is sometimes referred to as the **character arc**; that is, the movement of the character's development from the beginning of the script to the end.

One of the best, and most subtle, studies in character growth is in Bill Forsyth's film, *Local Hero*. Mac (Peter Riegert) works for Knox Oil and Gas in Houston. At the beginning of the film, Mac is isolated from his colleagues. He's more comfortable talking to people on the phone than dealing with them in person. He lives a controlled life: he's obsessively neat, drives a Porsche, lives in an exclusive high–rise, and values money and technology. When his company sends him to a small Scottish seaside village to

acquire the town for a future oil refinery, his behavior subtly changes over time. During his first few days there, he avoids the townspeople and restlessly walks on the beach in his suit and tie, briefcase at his side. As the place and the people begin to beguile him, he gradually changes. The changes are signaled in small visual details: he loosens his tie, then stops wearing a tie; unbuttons his suit coat, then begins wearing sweaters; takes off his shoes and walks barefoot on the beach; loses his watch on the beach without noticing; brings seashells back to his room and smells the salt water; gazes at the Northern Lights and drinks with his newfound friends. Finally, when he returns to Houston, he seems a stranger in his own home as he places a call to his friends in Scotland. He is a changed man.[8]

Another character who goes through similar, subtle changes is Shirley Valentine from the film of the same name. Shirley (Pauline Collins) is a frumpy British housewife who caters to the every need of her husband and grown daughter. When she has an opportunity to vacation in Greece with Jane (Alison Steadman), one of her friends, she surprises herself and everyone else by going. When she arrives in Greece, Jane promptly deserts her for a man, and Shirley is left to fend for herself. At first she wanders aimlessly, adrift in a strange land. Soon the sea and sun relax her and she sheds her proper British skin, revealing a girlish, carefree self. She is seduced by a native man, Costas (Tom Conti), who takes her out on his boat. They go skinny-dipping and make wild love. Shirley is infatuated with her new lover and when she discovers he plays this game with other female tourists, she laughs at herself and remains friends with him. Costas arranges for Shirley to waitress in a café by the sea, and she falls into the rhythms of the land and the people. When her husband grows impatient because she has not returned to England, he travels to Greece to find her; she is so changed he doesn't even recognize her. Shirley remains her own person and lets her husband do the catering this time.[9]

Perhaps the most subtle character arc in recent memory is that of Melvin Udall (Jack Nicholson) from *As Good As It Gets* (Oscar and Golden Globe Award for Best Original Screenplay as well as Best Acting Oscars for Jack Nicholson and Helen Hunt). At the beginning of the story, obsessive-compulsive Melvin Udall is a belligerent loner whose only contact with the world comes in the form of insults or cruel pranks (such as throwing his neighbor's dog down the garbage chute). As the story progresses, Melvin is gradually drawn out of his clandestine writer's existence. Little by little, Melvin takes small steps (as long as he doesn't step on the sidewalk cracks) away from his apartment into the world. He's befriended by a sympathetic waitress, Carol (Helen Hunt), who tolerates his rudeness when no one else will. He's further pulled from his controlled world when his neighbor, Simon (Greg Kinnear), a gay artist, is savagely beaten. Melvin takes care of Simon's dog (yes, the same one he threw down the garbage chute) while Simon recovers in the hospital. When Carol's son, who has an asthmatic

condition, grows seriously ill, Melvin employs a private doctor and pays all the bills. These character changes come slowly, almost indiscernibly, since Melvin complains bitterly even while he's helping. It isn't evident that he's able to move beyond his own selfishness and obsession until the end of the story as he accepts Simon for who he is and summons the courage to consider sharing his life with Carol.[10]

Usually, the character arc implies character growth. Yet change need not always be in an upward or positive direction. Some characters fall from grace or descend into their own personal nightmares. Remember Willard (Martin Sheen) from *Apocalypse Now*? The deeper he travels into the heart of the jungle, the more his state of mind deteriorates. By the time he reaches Kurtz's outpost, he wonders who has descended into greater madness—himself or Kurtz. When Kurtz utters his last words, "the horror, the horror," Willard realizes that he has fully entered the heart of darkness.[11]

Another bittersweet character arc is that of Dr. Malcolm Crowe (Bruce Willis) in M. Night Shyamalan's *The Sixth Sense*. Dr. Crowe is a respected child psychologist happily married to Anna (Olivia Williams). Early in the story, an intruder confronts Malcolm and Anna. The intruder is Vincent Gray (Donnie Wahlberg), one of Malcolm's former child patients, now an embittered adult, who suddenly shoots Malcolm. The story flashes forward two years. Malcolm is working with a new patient, Cole Sear (Haley Joel Osment), a troubled child who lives with his mother, Lynn (Toni Collette). As Malcolm begins to unravel Cole's secret, Anna grows increasingly distant, which perplexes Malcolm. He even fears she may be having an affair. Finally, Malcolm learns Cole's secret—he sees people who are dead. Malcolm eventually helps Cole live with his strange gift and in doing so discovers his own truth: he, too, is dead. As Malcolm reconstructs the events of his life since the shooting, he slowly comes to terms with his own mortality.[12]

It's not always possible or necessary to identify with a character. If a character is evocative enough, the audience will be compelled to want to know more. A good example of a character with whom it's difficult to identify or empathize, but who holds your interest nonetheless, is Dr. Hannibal Lecter (Anthony Hopkins) from *The Silence of the Lambs*. His sheer malevolence, obvious genius, and careful manipulation of Clarice Starling (Jody Foster) create both disgust and fascination among viewers. He is a complex character who exhibits little change throughout the story but who captivates and sustains the interest of the viewer nonetheless.[13]

If it's not necessary to identify with every character, is it necessary for every character to have a backstory? What about representational characters or characters who serve a larger purpose in the development of the work as a whole?

REPRESENTATIONAL CHARACTERS

Some characters are **representational**; that is, they are intentionally created as one-dimensional characters or characters utilized to reflect the theme of the work. Cartoon characters like Dick Tracy and Superman are obvious representational characters. Though these characters have some backstory, their histories aren't as important as their heroic characteristics. These characters are meant to be prototypical heroes who act as catalysts for action in the story. But don't be fooled—some cartoon characters, like the Simpson family, are far more dimensional than many live-action characters. You can't assume that a cartoon character will automatically be representational or that a live-action character will be dimensional.

Forrest Gump (Tom Hanks) could be considered a representational character. Because he only has an IQ of seventy-five, he sees the world as an innocent. Though Forrest's character changes very little throughout the story, his disarming, straightforward manner and lack of cynicism deeply affect those with whom he interacts, especially his childhood friend, Jenny (Robin Wright). He even manages to alter the course of history when he meets with historical figures ranging from Elvis Presley to John F. Kennedy.[14]

Another classic example of a representational character is that of Chance (Peter Sellers) in Jerzy Kosinski's novel and script (co-authored by Robert C. Jones) *Being There*. Chance, a simple-minded gardener who is also an innocent, is deliberately conceived as a representational character. Unable to form his own perceptions, he sees the world through the frame of the television set. All of his existence is meaningless unless it's validated on television. When he is accidentally hit by a limousine, Eve (Shirley MacLaine), the owner of the limo, takes Chance to her home to care for him. Chance passively allows himself to be taken in. Even when Eve mistakes his name as Chauncey Gardiner, he doesn't correct her. His character is imposed upon him by the characters who surround him. In that regard, he represents whatever other characters perceive him to be; he becomes what they need, whether it be a lover or a politician.[15]

Nor is it by chance that his name is Chance. Chance finds him standing on the curb watching televisions on display as he's hit by the limo. Chance brings him to Eve's attention. Chance creates a situation in which a feeble-minded man is perceived by all around him as a clever guru.

Names often have symbolic meaning in stories. In *Local Hero*, the two main women characters, Stella and Marina, represent the stars and the sea—the essence of the place. If you want your characters' names to have special significance within your story, you might want to buy a few baby name books. Sometimes you can find small, inexpensive ones at the checkout counters of grocery or discount stores. There are even specialized books for specific ethnic or cultural groups. Generally, these books provide you

with the name, its origin, and a list of nicknames derived from the name. You can also use the phone book as a source for brainstorming names. Whatever names you choose for your characters, make sure the names truthfully represent them.

INTRODUCING YOUR CHARACTER

As your story takes shape, you need to introduce each character within the context of the story. Introducing a character within the script is easier said than done. When you first introduce your character, you need to give an impression of the character's physical presence and capture the character's essence without narrowing your description too precisely. If your description is too broad, it will be difficult for a reader to imagine the character; if your description is too specific, it will be difficult for a casting agent to cast the role.

A good character description need not be lengthy to create an immediate impression of the character. In *Butch Cassidy and the Sundance Kid,* William Goldman quickly but adeptly introduces a girl moving up behind Butch in one simple line, "She is reasonably pretty, a little used."[16] Though the language is sparse, in an instant the description articulates all you need to know about this character.

Another accurate though brief description is the introduction of Lilly in Donald Westlake's *The Grifters* (based on the novel by Jim Thompson). Read the description and see if you could write a more complete description in as few words. "AN ANGLE through the open driver-side window of the Chrysler at LILLY DILLON (Anjelica Huston), 39 but looking younger, beautiful but cold and watchful."[17]

Sometimes it's impossible to separate a character from a sidekick or an item associated with the character. In Spike Lee's script *Do The Right Thing,* the description of Radio Raheem treats his radio as if it were an appendage of his body.

> In the BG, we hear the dum–dum–dum of a giant box. The sound gets louder as the box gets closer. The youths look down the block and see a tall young man coming towards them. He has a very distinct walk, it's more like a bop. This is RADIO RAHEEM (Bill Nunn). The size of his box is tremendous and one has to think how does he carry something that big around with him? It must weigh a ton, and it seems like the sidewalk shakes as the rap music blares out. The song we hear is the only one Radio Raheem plays.[18]

The environment and the objects with which characters interact or surround themselves provide further definition for characters. In James Schamus's screenplay *The Ice Storm,* (based on Rick Moody's novel), observe

how Paul is quickly characterized through the environment and his choice of reading material. He's on a train traveling from New York City to New Canaan, Connecticut. "On Paul Hood, 15-and-a-half, stoner-preppie look, hunched up in his seat under the faint emergency light. He reads his *Fantastic Four* comic book by the pale light of the emergency exit sign."[19]

On occasion, there are advantages to drawing out the description while drawing in the audience toward the mystery of the character. In *Edward Scissorhands*, Caroline Thompson leads you toward Edward (Johnny Depp) so that the viewer, like the inimitable Avon lady, Peg Boggs (Dianne Wiest), is both curious and repelled.

Peg has seen the outline of a man in the distant shadows. He's "jumpy, his movements erratic, unpredictable, and therefore dangerous." Peg catches a glimpse of light off his hands, there's something metallic, maybe a knife. Peg reassures him that she won't hurt him. Notice the tension and humor in the unfolding description that's interspersed with Peg's dialogue.

She makes her way across the attic, squinting at the figure.

> PEG
> Why are you hiding back
> there? You can't possibly be
> afraid of me. I'm an Avon
> sales representative. I'm as
> harmless as a cherry pie.

The man in the shadows stirs and is caught more distinctly by the shaft of dust-filled sunlight that shines through one of the grimy windows. He does indeed seem to be holding something--shears a full foot long. They belong, of course, to Edward Scissorhands.

At the sight of the blades, it's Peg's turn to gasp. Her coaxing turns to hysterical babble. She backs quickly away.

> PEG
> I can see now that I've
> disturbed you. How stupid
> of me. Don't be angry. I
> wouldn't hurt you, so it
> wouldn't be fair for you to
> hurt me. I'm going now.
> You'll be alone again. You
> can pretend I was never here.

```
                     Just stay where you are. I'll
                     be gone in a jiffy.
```

Edward tips his head forward inquiringly. It too is
now in the light.

```
                          EDWARD
                         (timid)
                        Don't go.
```

His hair is wildly trimmed, his face a topographical
map of ditches, pockmarks, gulleys, and gashes. His
eyes are so big they seem like two huge unfathomable
pools.[20]

Thompson creates "the need to know" as she simultaneously heightens tension in the scene.

All of these descriptions should give you a sense of how difficult it is to write concise character descriptions that capture the essence of the characters. In the past few years, character descriptions have become more terse. Sometimes, the only frame of reference is the character's age and gender. Whether your character introductions are painstakingly developed or simply stated, capturing the essence of any character is one of the most difficult challenges of shaping a memorable story. Giving definition and life to your characters will be easier once you're more familiar with the process of writing dialogue.

Try writing a description of the character you created earlier. Would a casting director have a hard time casting the character based on your description? If you were casting the film, whom would you choose to play your character?

REFERENCES

1. George Hickenlooper, ed., *Reel Conversations: Candid Interviews with Films' Foremost Directors and Critics*, Carol Publishing Company, New York, 1991, p. 149.
2. William Froug, *Zen and the Art of Screenwriting: Insights and Interviews*, Silman-James Press, Beverly Hills, 1996, p. 17.
3. Jim Uhls, *Fight Club*, Fox 2000 Pictures, 1999.
4. Margaret Mehring, *The Screenplay: A Blend of Film Form and Content*, Focal Press, Boston, 1990, p. 195.
5. Linda Seger, *Creating Unforgettable Characters*, Henry Holt and Company, New York, 1990, p. 5.

6. Maynard Allington, "A Matter of Character," *The Writer*, October 1998, pp. 23–24.
7. Denny Martin Flinn, *How Not to Write a Screenplay: 101 Common Mistakes Most Screenwriters Make*, Lone Eagle Publishing, Los Angeles, 1999, pp. 189–190.
8. Bill Forsyth, *Local Hero*, Warner Bros., 1983.
9. Willy Russell, *Shirley Valentine*, Paramount, 1989.
10. Mark Andrus and James L. Brooks, *As Good As It Gets*, TriStar Pictures/Gracie Films, 1997.
11. Francis Ford Coppola and John Milius, *Apocalypse Now*, United Artists, 1979.
12. M. Night Shyamalan, *The Sixth Sense*, Spyglass Entertainment/Hollywood Pictures, 1999.
13. Ted Tally, *The Silence of the Lambs* (based on the novel by Thomas Harris), Orion, 1990.
14. Eric Roth, *Forrest Gump* (based on the novel by Winston Groom), Paramount Pictures, 1994.
15. Jerzy Kosinski and Robert C. Jones, *Being There* (based on the novel by Jerzy Kosinski), Lorimar Productions, 1979.
16. William Goldman, *Butch Cassidy and the Sundance Kid*, Campanile Productions and 20th Century Fox, 1969.
17. Donald E. Westlake, *The Grifters* (based on Jim Thompson's novel), Miramax, 1990.
18. Spike Lee, *Do The Right Thing*, Universal City Studios, 1989.
19. James Schamus, *The Ice Storm: The Shooting Script*, Newmarket Press, New York, 1997, p. 1.
20. Caroline Thompson, *Edward Scissorhands*, 20th Century Fox, 1990.

8

Crafting Dialogue

Mrs. Robinson, if you don't mind my saying so, this conversation is getting a little strange.

—Benjamin (Dustin Hoffman) to Mrs. Robinson
(Anne Bancroft) in *The Graduate*[1]

Conversation, an exchange unique to human beings, is equally capable of luring us toward one another as it is of casting us away from one another. Whether conversation is mundane or profound, restorative or destructive, its pervasive nature weaves a tapestry of talk into our daily lives. In bus stations, prisons, alleys, shacks, coffee houses, offices, banks, fast food restaurants, grocery store lines, backyards, kitchens—every place inhabited by people—conversation flourishes.

You'd think that being amidst people, hearing them prattle around you every day, would empower you to write great dialogue. Yet well-crafted dialogue is far more elusive than you might imagine. Dialogue is not recorded conversation; it is carefully constructed language created to reveal characterization, advance the plot, evoke mood, heighten tension, and provoke thought.

Before you can write compelling dialogue, you should read compelling dialogue. Shakespeare is a good start. Try writing trenchant dialogue in iambic pentameter and you'll begin to appreciate his genius. You might also read contemporary masters like Harold Pinter, Sam Shepard, and Tom Stoppard. Playwrights are great models since plays rely almost totally upon dialogue to convey story.

One of the most powerful uses of dialogue in recent literature is in the novel *Interviewing Matisse or The Woman Who Died Standing Up* by Lily Tuck. In an all-night phone conversation, Molly and Lily babble in tangents ranging from death to Matisse. Even though the story is told in the

first person, you feel as if you're secretly listening to other people on the party line.

> I said, "We saw *East of Eden.*"
> Molly said, "Oh, with James Dean."
> I said, "Julie Harris was in it, too. Remember how the two of them kissed on the Ferris wheel?—but what were we talking about, Molly?"
> Molly said, "Bibi—poor Bibi flunking her biology test."
> I said, "At least Bibi is getting an education. Nowadays, all you hear on television is how badly educated American kids are—oh, and what was the word you used, Molly? Not *palimpsest*, the other one? *Innumerate.* Yes, how innumerate the kids today are. One of the kids I heard said he thought Chernobyl was Cher's real name and the District of Columbia, he said, was some place in Central America. Makes you think, doesn't it? . . ."[2]

I hope so. Good dialogue should make you think. Thinking about the meaning of language and the purpose of conversation also helps you generate lively, thoughtful dialogue. If you examine real language usage, you'll come closer to understanding how humans communicate and to recognizing the differences between real language and constructed language.

One person who has thought a great deal about how people converse with one another is Dr. Deborah Tannen. Her linguistic research, published in works like *That's Not What I Meant: How Conversational Style Makes or Breaks Relationships, You Just Don't Understand*, and *Talking from 9 to 5: Women and Men in the Workplace: Language, Sex and Power*, explores the dynamics of women and men in conversation. Her research is valuable to writers because it reveals many of the sources of conflict among humans. Consider this conversation. A woman wakes a man up in the middle of the night.

> HE: What's wrong?
> SHE: You were taking up too much of the bed.
> HE: I'm sorry.
> SHE: You're always doing that.
> HE: What?
> SHE: Taking advantage of me.
> HE: Wait a minute. I was asleep. How can you hold me responsible for what I do when I'm asleep?

The woman then proceeds to elaborate instances of previous perceived offenses.

Dr. Tannen uses this example to talk about "metamessages," representative messages about the relationship between people and their attitudes toward one another. Dr. Tannen's reading of the woman's responses

is that the woman felt that the man generally took advantage of her, taking up too much of her "space."[3]

The metamessage in real language works very much like subtext in literary language. **Subtext** represents the message residing below the surface of the words, signifying the marrow of the tension. Ostensibly the conversation is about physical space but the real message comes from inside the woman's pain.

The best dialogue fools you, makes you believe that each character is speaking spontaneously in response to another character's thoughts or actions. Well-crafted dialogue gives you a sense of intimacy and immediacy, as if you're eavesdropping on other people's conversations.

Masterful dialogue is dialogue that sounds like real language. But what does real language sound like? How does real language compare to dialogue? You can truly appreciate how fantastic the illusion is if you eavesdrop on a real conversation. The following conversation is excerpted from a conversation between two young men taped and transcribed by one of my former students, Jim Gunshanan. Read the conversation and jot down any observations you might have.

J: Um . . . yeah, do you think I should get a flower or somethin' for um . . .
B: Definitely.
J: . . . Julia?
B: Definitely. Absolutely.
J: Yeah. (Pause) You know what I was thinkin', actually, um, was getting her the . . . well this might be a little over-ambitious for like a present kinda thing, but, ah, I was thinkin' 'bout getting her the, ah, *Complete Works of Shakespeare* . . .
B: No.
J: . . . Book, you know? Okay. (Laughs)
B: Krista told me about this, she said . . .
J: I know, I . . .
B: . . . that, uh, she saw your *Complete Works of Shakespeare* and all this stuff, and . . .
J: Mmm hmm.
B: And, um, and you said, "Do you think I oughta . . ." "No, Jim!"
J: (Laughs)
B: And then that's as far as your—
J: I know, that's all . . . I didn't even say, I was, I said, um, yeah, I kinda was deciding, 'cause I mean, there's a difference between getting somebody a flower . . .
B: Wanna Pringle?
J: No, and getting somebody a twenty dollar . . .
B: It's not corn, is it?
J: . . . book. No, I just don't feel like eat—I just had a big lunch. But, um, I even, she didn't, I didn't even have to finish my sentence, I just said, um, "Hey Krista, I know this might," what'd I say, okay, "Hey Krista, I

know you're probably gonna say no to this, but just hear me out. I was thinkin' about buying her the . . ." she just goes, "No!"
B: (Laughs)
J: 'Cause she saw me lookin' at the book, she was like, "I don't think so."
B: D–Does she know that she wanted one, did Krista know?
J: Yeah, 'cause I told her, I said well, it's not just, it wouldn't just be like an arbitrary stupid gift, I mean, she said she wanted to get it, so—
B: Mmm hmm. No. Nah, just get, just get her like (pause) either one or half a dozen flowers.
J: Half a dozen? What the hell for? That's kind of a weird choice. "One or half a dozen."
B: One or, uhhh, three hundred. (Laughs)
J: (Laughs) I know, what the hell is that?
B: Well, uh, that, I mean, a dozen is far too many, I mean, uh, that's like . . .
J: Well, I think one . . .

Though the conversation continued for some time, you should be able to draw some conclusions from this excerpt. What, if anything, did you observe about real language? Did you notice any patterns? Was the conversation interesting? Did you learn anything about the speakers from the conversation? Would this conversation work as dialogue in a scene? If not, why not?

Try to rewrite the transcribed conversation as a scene. Feel free to embellish the characterization and language in any way you'd like. You can add to or omit wherever necessary. Remember that a scene should have a beginning, middle, and end, an event or interaction, and tension. After you've written the scene, write about what you discovered in the process of writing the real language as a scene.

Now that you've discovered some characteristics of real language, how do you think constructed language differs from real language? What characteristics are distinctive to dialogue? In order to write dialogue well, you need to be aware of the differences between naturalistic and stylized dialogue and develop the ability to employ each as needed for the character and circumstances.

NATURALISTIC DIALOGUE

Naturalistic dialogue is dialogue that appears to emulate natural spoken language but is in essence carefully contrived language. Characteristics of

naturalistic dialogue include the use of informal, vernacular speech, slang, profanity, and **overlapping dialogue** (when two or more people speak at the same time). Since today's culture is largely informal, much of the dialogue in contemporary American scripts utilizes naturalistic dialogue. Typically, most characters speak naturalistically unless they're in a majestic, historical, formal, or professional setting or unless they're under duress and exhibiting uncharacteristic behavior.

Naturalistic dialogue establishes the credibility of characters, especially those characters with whom the intended audience might closely identify. Naturalistic dialogue is essential in a script that attempts to authentically depict "real" people.

Colloquialisms may be used to accentuate the natural cadence of language, especially when you want to represent speech patterns found in particular parts of the country. In the Coen brothers' film *Fargo* (Oscar for Best Original Screenplay), the northern Minnesota and North Dakota locations seem especially authentic since the characters repeatedly use the vernacular, typically in phrases like "you're darn tootin'" or "you bet, yah." In the following scene, Marge (Frances McDormand, Oscar for Best Actress), a very pregnant police officer, questions two hookers. Marge's unassuming manner creates trust in others and credibility in her character. Much of her character's charm as well as the humor in the scene is created through the dialogue. Notice how the repetition, peppered with colloquialisms, emulates the cadence of the region.

```
                   MARGE
          Okay, I want you to tell me
          what these fellas looked like.

                   HOOKER ONE
          Well, the little guy, he was
          kinda funny-looking.

                   MARGE
          In what way?

                   HOOKER ONE
          I dunno. Just funny-looking.

                   MARGE
          Can you be any more specific?

                   HOOKER ONE
          I really couldn't say. He
          wasn't circumcised.

                   MARGE
          Was he funny-looking apart
          from that?
```

        HOOKER ONE
Yah.

        MARGE
So you were having sex with
the little fella, then?

        HOOKER ONE
Uh-huh.

        MARGE
Is there anything else you
can tell me about him?

        HOOKER ONE
No. Like I say, he was funny-
looking. More'n most people
even.

        MARGE
And what about the other
fella?

        HOOKER TWO
He was a little older. Looked
like the Marlboro man.

        MARGE
Yah?

        HOOKER TWO
Yah. Maybe I'm sayin' that
'cause he smoked Marlboros.

        MARGE
Uh-huh.

        HOOKER TWO
A subconscious-type thing.

        MARGE
Yah, that can happen.

        HOOKER TWO
Yah.

        HOOKER ONE
They said they were goin' to
the Twin Cities.

        MARGE
Oh, yah?

                    HOOKER TWO
        Yah.

                    HOOKER ONE
        Yah. Is that useful to ya?

                    MARGE
        Oh, you bet, yah.[4]

Another use of dialogue that helps to define character and enhance familiarity with the character is the use of a "catch phrase." This is an expression that's frequently repeated by the character and ultimately associated with the character. In Billy Bob Thornton's *Sling Blade* (Oscar for Best Original Screenplay), the lead character, Karl (Billy Bob Thornton), repeatedly uses the phrase "all right then." Karl is a simple-minded man who's been institutionalized for a criminal act he committed in his youth. When he's released into the world as an adult, he's easily intimidated by others. The phrase "all right then" exemplifies his agreeable though inarticulate nature. He's at ease with Frank (Lucas Black), a young boy who's equally alienated by the adult world. Frank finds Karl's simple nature and speech reassuring. In the following scene, Frank and Karl sit at night in Frank's secret place. Frank interrupts the silence with which they're both comfortable.

                    FRANK
        I'm getting' tired of readin'
        for awhile.

                    KARL
        All right then.

                    FRANK
        Boy, folks sure had it rough
        back a long time ago, didn't
        they?

                    KARL
        Yeah, I reckon they did. Hit
        like to tore me up when I
        read about that pore little
        cripple boy.

                    FRANK
        Yeah, me too. (*pause*) That
        was nice of that woman to
        give you them flowers.

```
                    KARL
          Hit was right thoughty of her.

                    FRANK
          I was wantin' to ask you
          somethin'.

                    KARL
          All right then.⁵
```

Earlier in the story, Frank expresses how comforted he is by Karl's manner of speaking. Frank's father is dead and his abusive stepfather scares him. Frank joins Karl in the garage where he's eating one of his favorite foods—canned meat.

```
                    FRANK
          I'd like to kill that son of
          a bitch. I hate him.

                    KARL
          You ort not to talk that way.
          You're just a boy.

                    FRANK
          Well, I hate him.

                    KARL
          He ort not to talk that away
          to you neither. He ain't no
          count. He's mean to you and
          your mama. (pause) Yore mama
          and that feller that's carryin'
          me to get somethin' d'eat's
          gonna be back here directly.

                    FRANK
          Will you stay here with us
          for a long time?

                    KARL
          I reckon if you want me to.
          (pause) I got some of that
          potted meat and sodie
          crackers left over if you
          want some.

                    FRANK
          I don't see how you can eat
          that stuff with all those
          insides it's made out of.
```

>   KARL
> I reckon it tastes pretty
> good to me.
>
>   FRANK
> I like the way you talk.
>
>   KARL
> I like the way you talk.[6]

The repetition works well as a structuring device to deepen the burgeoning relationship between Frank and Karl.

Structuring dialogue within a scene is much trickier than it would appear to be. Once again, the Coen brothers provide a good example. In *Blood Simple*, what appears to be a naturalistic interchange is really a meticulously structured **set-up** for a powerful **tag** or **punch line**, a line that acts as a **payoff** at the culmination of the scene. The set-up/payoff structure is frequently used in comedy, but its use in this scene demonstrates how effectively if can be used to build tension in drama.

Julian Marty (Dan Hedaya), the owner of a seedy bar, has hired Loren Visser (M. Emmet Walsh), a sleazy P.I., to find out if his wife, Abby (Frances McDormand), is cheating on him. Visser goes to Marty's office at the bar to collect his money for a job well done, too well done, from Marty's point of view. Visser slaps pictures of Abby in action in front of Marty, and Marty doesn't appreciate the "fringe benefit." He wanted information, not graphics. In his anger, Marty sets up the impetus for the subsequent dialogue when he tells Visser that "in Greece they cut off the head of the messenger who brought the bad news." Visser responds.

>   VISSER
> Well first off, Julian, I
> don't know what the story is
> in Greece but in this state
> we got very definite laws
> about that . . .

> Marty, hunched over the standing safe behind his
> desk, tosses in the photograph and takes out a pay
> envelope.

>   VISSER (cont.)
> . . . Second place I ain't a
> messenger, I'm a private
> investigator. And third place
> --and most important--it ain't
> such bad news. I mean you

> thought he was
> colored . . .
> (he laughs)
> . . . You're always assumin'
> the worst . . .

Visser blows another smoke ring, pushes a fat finger
through the middle of it, and beams at Marty.

> VISSER (cont.)
> . . . Anything else?

> MARTY
> Yeah, don't come by here any
> more. If I need you again I
> know which rock to turn over.

Marty scales the pay envelope across the desk. It
hits Visser in the chest and bounces to the floor.

Visser looks stonily down at the envelope; no
expression for a beat. Then he roars with laughter.

> VISSER
> That's good . . . "which rock
> to turn over" . . . that's very
> good . . .

Sighing, he leans forward to pick up the envelope.
He rises, straightens his cowboy hat, and walks over
to a screen door letting out on the bar's back
parking lot.

> VISSER
> Well, gimme a call whenever
> you wanna cut off my head . . .

He pauses at the door, cocks his head, then turns
back to the desk and picks up his cigarette lighter.
Returning to the door:

> VISSER (cont.)
> . . . I can crawl around
> without it.[7]

The payoff for the setup works because the characters and their respective dialogue are so convincing, and though the whole scene is carefully
contrived, the audience never feels manipulated.

The more naturalistic the dialogue, the greater the opportunity for building tension within a scene. In the following scene from John Singleton's *Boyz in the Hood*, notice the difference between the teacher's dialogue and that of her students. In this scene, Mrs. Olaf (Susan Falcon), a "skinny frayed haired white lady in her mid-forties," is irritated with Tre (Desi Arnez Hines II), a fifth grader who has disrupted class with his comedic behavior. The dialogue helps to build tension within the scene while the comedic nature of the character simultaneously disperses the tension, at least in the beginning of the scene.

> MRS. OLAF
> Would <u>you</u> like to teach the
> class?

The class goes "Oooh!" at this challenge.

> TRE
> Yeah, I can do that.

Mrs. Olaf is surprised.

> MRS. OLAF
> Very well then, come up here
> . . . and instruct us.

Tre cooly walks up to the map. Nearby Bobby (Valentino Harrison) sits. It is evident that he is jealous. Tre has caught the attention of the entire class.

> TRE
> (cooly)
> Can I have that?
> (indicating the pointer)

Tre begins to speak but not before Mrs. Olaf stops him.

> MRS. OLAF
> What will be the basis of
> your lecture?

> TRE
> What?

> MRS. OLAF
> (enunciating)
> What are you going to talk
> about?

> TRE
> I'm gonna tell you if you
> let me talk! Shoot!

The class laughs.

>   TRE
>   Okay. Alright, does anybody
>   know what the name of this
>   place is?

The pointer is on the continent of Africa.

>   TRINA
>   That's Africa, I know that.

>   TRE
>   That's right, that's Africa.
>   But did you know that Africa
>   is the place where they found
>   the body of the first man?

>   BOBBY
>   Yeah, I know dat. I heard it
>   in a song once.

>   TRE
>   My daddy says that makes it
>   the place where all people
>   originated from, that means
>   everybody is really from
>   Africa.
>   (gestures with pointer)
>   Everybody, all of y'all,
>   everybody.

>   BOBBY
>   I ain't from Africa, I'm from
>   Crenshaw Mafia!

He throws up a gang sign.

>   TRE
>   Like it or not you from
>   Africa.

>   BOBBY
>   I ain't from no Africa. You
>   from Africa! You African
>   booty scratcher![8]

Singleton's script captures the realities of life for the adolescents growing up in South Central Los Angeles.

In Allison Anders' script (based on Richard Peck's novel *Don't Look and It Won't Hurt*), *Gas—Food—Lodging*, naturalistic dialogue dominates the narrative and heightens the tension between the characters. In this scene, seventeen-year-old Trudi (Ione Skye) has just found out that she's pregnant. She and her mother, Nora (Brooke Adams), a struggling waitress in her late thirties, eat at an outdoor table at a Dairy Queen.

               NORA
Who's the father?

               TRUDI
I don't know.

               NORA
Nice.

               TRUDI
A guy, okay? A jerk.

               NORA
Well, we need to sit down
with this jerk and talk over
the details.

               TRUDI
If you can find him. I have
nothing to say to him.

               NORA
Be practical. He has to pay
for it, it's only fair.
You're the one who has to go
through the abortion, it's
the least he can do.

               TRUDI
Abortion? I haven't even
decided yet what I'm gonna do.

               NORA
There's nothing to decide,
Trudi. You have no choice.

               TRUDI
Bullshit! I have options! You
can't tell me!

Nora begins cleaning up the trash from the table.

> NORA
> You gonna finish that?

Trudi pushes the food, aggressively out of her face.

> TRUDI
> This is my body! You can't
> tell me what to do!

> NORA
> I'm not even going to discuss
> this with you.

Nora walks to the car. Trudi follows her, in a rage.
AT THE CAR Nora opens the door as Trudi rants.

> TRUDI
> Guess you don't want me to
> make the same mistake you
> made--right? You wish you'd
> had an abortion instead of
> having me, right? Life woulda
> been easier for you without
> me, just fucking say it, Mom!

> NORA
> That's enough, Trudi! Get in
> the car!

> TRUDI
> You probably even tried to
> abort me, didn't you?

CLOSE ON Nora's face, anguished by her daughter's
cruel accusations. She gets in the car. She turns on
the engine and sits. She gets out of the running
car, with her purse and starts walking.[9]

The candid dialogue between mother and daughter reveals a dichotomy of closeness and distance, attention and tension, and an almost palpable pain.

As you write, you'll find that naturalistic dialogue isn't always suitable for the character or circumstances. You may find stylized dialogue more appropriate for a character or specific scene.

STYLIZED DIALOGUE

Stylized dialogue incorporates elements of literary or artistic expression within the dialogue. The characteristics of stylized dialogue include formal

language that may have identifiable patterns, such as repetition; meter or rhyme; highly literate, intellectual language; and poetic, figurative language.

Stylized dialogue is likely to be uttered by characters who narrate the story, who are godlike or represent royalty, who use English as a second language, who represent a more formal historical period, who work in a profession such as teaching or preaching where they are expected to speak formally, who are suddenly and unpredictably passionate or violent, or who are delusional or have delusions of grandeur.

In the timeless classic *The Wizard of Oz*, the Wizard (referred to as Oz in the script and played by Frank Morgan) uses formal, figurative language to heighten his majestic presence and to intimidate Dorothy (Judy Garland) and her companions. In this scene, the Wizard's dialogue utilizes both alliteration (repetition of consonants or initial sounds in adjacent words) and assonance (repetition of vowels).

OZ
Step forward, Tin Man!

(the Tin Man (Jack Haley), who is trembling so hard his joints rattle, is shoved a pace forward by the others)

OZ (contd)
You dare to come to me for a heart--do you? You clinking, clanking, clabbering, collection of caliginous junk!

TIN MAN
Yes--sir--Your honor . . .

OZ
And you . . . Scarecrow . . .

(the Scarecrow (Ray Bolger) is pushed forward by the lion, (Bert Lahr))

OZ (contd)
. . . have the effrontery to ask for a brain? You billowing bale of bovine fodder![10]

In Paddy Chayefsky's Academy-Award-winning script *Network*, Howard Beale (Peter Finch), an aging television news anchorman, is losing his mind. The executive profiteers at the station have decided to capitalize on Howard's vulnerability by donning him the "mad prophet of the

airways." Every week, the cameras turn on Howard as he rants and raves before millions of viewers. Read this excerpt from one of Howard's monologues. See if you recognize the elements of stylized language present in Howard's speech.

```
              HOWARD
     . . . Television is not the
     truth! Television is a
     goddamned amusement park,
     that's what television is!
     Television is a circus, a
     carnival, a travelling troupe
     of acrobats and story-tellers,
     singers and dancers, jugglers,
     side-show freaks, lion-tamers
     and football players. We're in
     the boredom killing business!
     If you want the truth, go to
     God, go to your guru, go to
     yourself because that's the
     only place you'll ever find any
     real truth! But, man, you're
     never going to get any truth
     from us. We'll tell you any-
     thing you want to hear. We lie
     like hell! We'll tell you
     Kojak always gets the killer,
     and nobody ever gets cancer in
     Archie Bunker's house. And no
     matter how much trouble the
     hero is in, don't worry: just
     look at your watch--at the end
     of the hour, he's going to
     win. We'll tell you any shit
     you want to hear! We deal in
     illusion, man! None of it's
     true! But you people sit
     there--all of you--day after
     day, night after night, all
     ages, colors, creeds--we're
     all you know. You're beginning
     to believe the illusion we're
     spinning here . . .[11]
```

Because the dialogue is spoken by someone who's lost his mind, the formality and repetition present in this speech strongly support the characterization.

Another character whose mind works differently than that of the average person is Ricky Finn (Wes Bentley) from *American Beauty*. A sensitive, intense character who sees the world primarily through the lens of his video camera, he expresses his unique world view to Jane Burnham (Thora Birch) in the following scene. His poetic language is in keeping with his introverted and introspective character.

```
On VIDEO: We're in an empty parking lot on a cold,
gray day. Something is floating across from us . . .
it's an empty, wrinkled, white PLASTIC BAG. We
follow it as the wind carries it in a circle around
us, sometimes whipping it about violently, or,
without warning, sending it soaring skyward, then
letting it float gracefully down to the ground . . .

Jane and Ricky sit on the bed, watching his
WIDE-SCREEN TV.

                        RICKY
                It was one of those days when
                it's a minute away from
                snowing. And there's this
                electricity in the air, you
                can almost hear it, right? And
                this bag was just . . . dancing
                with me. Like a little kid
                beggin me to play with it. For
                fifteen minutes. That's the day
                I realized that there was this
                entire life behind things, and
                this incredibly benevolent
                force that wanted me to know
                there was no reason to be
                afraid. Ever.

A beat.

                        RICKY
                Video's a poor excuse, I
                know. But it helps me
                remember . . . I need to
                remember . . .

Now Jane is watching him.

                        RICKY
                    (distant)
                Sometimes there's so much
```

>   beauty in the world I feel
>   like I can't take it . . . and
>   my heart is going to cave
>   in.[12]

   Another example of highly stylized dialogue is found in *Shakespeare in Love* (Best Original Screenplay Oscar and Golden Globe, Best Screenplay-New York Critics Circle) by Marc Norman and Tom Stoppard. Because the story unfolds during the summer of 1593 in Elizabethan England, the stylized language is in keeping with the time and place. Notice how subtly and seamlessly the fictional Shakespeare's voice melds with contemporary humor in the following scene, when young Will Shakespeare (Joseph Fiennes) seeks counsel from Dr. Moth (Anthony Sher).

DR. MOTH sits by the couch, listening to WILL and occasionally making a note on a pad he holds on his knee. What we have here is nothing less than the false dawn of analysis. The session is being timed by an hourglass.

>   WILL
>   Words, words, words . . . once,
>   I had a gift . . . I could
>   make love out of words as a
>   potter makes cups out of clay
>   . . . love that overthrows
>   empires, love that binds two
>   hearts together come hellfire
>   and brimstone . . . for
>   sixpence a line, I could
>   cause a riot in a nunnery
>   . . . but now . . .
>
>   DR. MOTH
>   And yet you tell me you lie
>   with women?

Will seems unwilling to respond. Dr. Moth refers to his notes.

>   DR. MOTH
>   Black Sue, Fat Phoebe, Ros-
>   aline, Burbage's seamstress,
>   Aphrodite, who does it behind
>   the Dog and . . .

                    WILL
               (interrupting)
          Aye, now and again, but what
          of it? I have lost my gift.
               (not finding this easy)
          It's as if my quill is
          broken. As if the organ of
          the imagination has dried up.
          As if the proud tower of my
          genius has collapsed.

                    DR. MOTH
          Interesting.

                    WILL
          Nothing comes.

                    DR. MOTH
          Most interesting.

                    WILL
               (interrupting)
          It is like trying to pick a
          lock with a wet herring.[13]

Once you're able to discriminate between naturalistic and stylized dialogue, you'll have a better understanding of when each might be appropriate in the development of your story and characterization. It's important that you understand that a character's dialogue might shift back and forth between naturalistic and stylized dialogue. Changing factors such as mood and motivation or action and reaction, may alter the character's dialogue at any given time during the dialogue or during the course of the story.

A good example of how a character might shift back and forth between styles is found in John Patrick Shanley's *Moonstruck*. Loretta (Cher) has promised her fiancé, Johnny (Danny Aiello), who is in Italy with his dying mother, that she will try to mend the bad blood between Johnny and his brother, Ronny (Nicolas Cage). In this scene, Loretta meets Ronny for the first time in the basement of the bakery where he works. Notice how Ronny's language tends to shift between informality and formality, the banal and the poetic.

                    RONNY
          Have you come from my
          brother?

                    LORETTA
          Yes.

                    RONNY
          Why?

                    LORETTA
          I'm going to marry him.

                    RONNY
          You are going to marry my
          brother?

                    LORETTA
          Yes. Do you want . . .

                    RONNY
          I have no life.

                    LORETTA
          Excuse me.

                    RONNY
          I have no life. My brother
          Johnny took my life from me.

                    LORETTA
          I don't understand.

Everything in the oven room has stopped and everyone
is watching.

                    RONNY
          And now he's getting married.
          He has his, he's getting his.
          And he wants me to come? What
          is life?

He picks up the wooden spatula and slides it into
the oven.

                    LORETTA
          I didn't come here to upset
          you.

Ronny slides a bunch of loaves out of the oven on the
spatula, turns them around, and slides them back in.

                    RONNY
          They say bread is life. So I
          bake bread, bread, bread.

> (He's picking up loaves of
> bread from one of the boxes
> on the floor, and casually
> tossing them across the
> room.) And the years go by!
> By! By! And I sweat and
> shovel this stinkin dough in
> and outta this hot hole in
> the wall and I should be so
> happy, huh, sweetheart? You
> want me to come to the
> wedding of my brother
> Johnny?!! Where is my
> wedding? Chrissy! Over by the
> wall! Gimme the big knife![14]

Ronny is really a decent, deeply feeling human being who has been physically and spiritually wounded. When Loretta comes to see him, she triggers the hurt in him, stimulating a shift in language.

In Jim Uhl's *Fight Club*, the tone is darkly humorous and the dialogue primarily naturalistic. However, in the following scene, Marla, the queen of dysfunctional behavior, employs figurative language to describe her alienation. In keeping with her drug-induced persona, Marla's language borders on the surreal. Marla, hair disheveled, dressed in a ratty old dress, joins Jack, the narrator, in the kitchen.

Marla's FOOTSTEPS can be heard coming down the stairs.
JACK'S POV--as he really grinds the soap against the
pants, splashes water all over the place.

JACK'S POV PIVOTS, WIDEN ON ROOM. Marla enters.
Tyler is GONE. Jack looks around to the open back
door, then back at Marla. She lights a cigarette.

> JACK (V.O.)
> Except for their humping,
> Tyler and Marla were never in
> the same room. The same
> disappearing act my parents
> pulled for years--one came
> in, and the other was gone.

Marla moves very close to Jack and props a leg up
on a stack of magazines near him. She's not wearing
underwear. Jack becomes very aware of his having no
pants on, so he pushes up against the counter.

Marla lasciviously pulls the hemline further up her leg.

> MARLA
> I got this dress at a thrift
> store for one dollar.

> JACK
> It was worth every penny.

> MARLA
> It's a bridesmaid's dress.
> Someone loved it intensely for
> one day, then tossed it. Like
> a Christmas tree--so special,
> then, bam, it's on the side of
> the road with tinsel still
> clinging to it.[15]

By likening herself to a discarded Christmas tree, Marla's language is elevated and thus more stylized than the more naturalistic dialogue that pervades the script.

Another character who vacillates between the real and the surreal is that of Meryl (Laura Linney) from the highly inventive script, *The Truman Show*. In the story, Truman Burbank (Jim Carrey) is the victim of a media experiment. As the center of a twenty-four-hour "real world" show, Truman grows up in a fictitious town surrounded by actors who play his family and friends. His wife is Meryl, a pretty, perky actress who's managed to convince Truman they're happily married. As Truman begins to question his existence, his "relationships" begin to unravel. In the following scene, Meryl's dialogue slips back and forth between naturalistic dialogue when she's talking to Truman and highly stylized language when she's selling products to the audience of whom Truman is unaware.

> MERYL
> Let me get you some help,
> Truman. You're not well.

> TRUMAN
> (ignoring her medical advice)
> Why do you want to have a
> child with me? You can't
> stand me.

> MERYL
> That's not true.

Meryl picks up a package and holds it to camera.

> MERYL
> Why don't I make you some of
> this new Mococoa Drink? All
> natural. Cocoa beans from the
> upper slopes of Mount
> Nicaragua. No artificial
> sweeteners -
>
> TRUMAN
> (incredulous)
> - What the hell are you
> talking about?!
>
> MERYL
> I've tasted other cocoas.
> This is the best.[16]

One of America's master scriptwriters, Woody Allen, slips in and out of naturalistic and stylized dialogue flawlessly in the following excerpt from *Hannah and Her Sisters*. Mickey Sachs (Woody Allen), a chronic hypochondriac who believes he's near death, is sitting in the library surrounded by open tomes. The one in his hands reads: Schopenhauer.

> MICKEY
> (reads)
> The individual is simply the
> will to live personified.
> Although -
> (picking up another book)
> Hume says we're only a bundle
> of perceptions . . . This is
> not helping me . . .
> (lifts a third book)
> On the other hand, Spinoza
> figured the inner nature of
> the world is God . . . How does
> he know? These guys all think
> they figured it out . . . And
> all those materialists
> believed in total
> annihilation after death
> . . . Like the stoics . . . what
> the hell did the stoics know
> . . . sat around in white
>
> (MORE)

```
                    (MICKEY (contd)
           robes  and  took  public  baths
           . . . I'm gonna listen to guys
           who bathe together? . . . I
           mean common science
           . . . the conservation of
           matter . . . it's
           indestructible . . .
               (waving Schopenhauer)
           Schopenhauer said the will is
           imperishable . . . But the
           universe itself is of limited
           duration . . . so you got the
           will and no universe . . . where
           do you eat? Not according to
           Nietzsche . . . Eternal
           recurrence . . . everything is
           going to happen over and over
           exactly as it occurs . . .
           which means I will have to
           sit through the Ice Capades
           again! Not worth it . . .
```

CUT outside Library. Exiting.

```
                    MICKEY'S THOUGHTS
           All those philosophers.
           They're real deep when you're
           a student but when you're
           facing death--how shall I put
           it?--Mere words suck.[17]
```

Allen's dialogue epitomizes the character, fusing stylized and naturalized language together into a seamless whole.

CONTEXT

Dialogue does not exist in isolation; it should have a specific purpose within the context of the story. What immediately precedes a sequence of dialogue as well as what comes after may have special significance or impact upon the dialogue.

Remember the restaurant scene in *When Harry Met Sally . . .*? In her attempts to prove to Harry (Billy Crystal) that women can effectively fake an orgasm, Sally (Meg Ryan) performs a convincing simulation of an orgasm

while seated at the table in the restaurant. The line of dialogue that immediately follows this display is uttered by an older woman (Rob Reiner's mother, Estelle Reiner) seated in the restaurant who says to the waitress: "I'll have what she's having."[18] This line would have had no humor, would have been meaningless, in fact, had the line not been set up by the preceding action.

Another method of contextualizing humor is with a **running gag**, a phrase that's repeated throughout the script, each time in a new context. One of the classic running gags is found in William Goldman's *Butch Cassidy and the Sundance Kid*. For a better part of the story, the outlaw leaders of the Hole-in-the-Wall Gang, Butch and Sundance, are relentlessly pursued by a posse. From time to time along their journey Butch and Sundance stop and ask, "Who are those guys?"[19]

A more recent example is found in Hillary Henkin and David Mamet's script *Wag the Dog* (based on Larry Beinhard's novel *American Hero*). Stanley Moss, a penultimate Hollywood producer, is secretly commissioned by the U.S. government to "produce" a phony war via the media. Every time a complication arises, Stanley's refrain is, "Oh, this is nothing . . ." as he launches into his own "war" stories in the trenches of Hollywood.[20]

To really appreciate any running gag, you should see a film in its entirety, since running gags are structured to derive humor from the context of the whole script.

An example of how dialogue that could be interpreted as straight dialogue attains a humorous connotation through the setup of the previous action occurs in *My Cousin Vinny*, by Dale Launer. Two college kids, Bill Gambini (Ralph Macchio) and Stan Rothenstein (Mitchell Whitfield), have been arrested and mistakenly accused of killing a convenience store clerk. While they are in jail, a new guy comes to the cell. Bill is asleep so Stan has to handle it on his own. He's heard the tales of what happens to men in jail and he fears the worst.

```
                VINNY
      You must be Stan.
        (Extends his hand)
      How ya doin'?

                STAN
        (shrugs, cautiously shakes
        hand)
      Why'd they bring you in here?

                VINNY
      I just got in. I asked where
      the new guys were so they
      brought me here.
        (looks at Bill, fondly)
      Hey, he's sleepin', cute
      little guy.
```

Despite his raunchy appearance, Vinny's friendly--
which Stan misconstrues to be a cat playing with a
mouse. He avoids meeting Vinny's eyes.

> STAN
>
> I . . . don't want to . . .
> do this.

> VINNY
>
> I don't blame you, if I was in
> your situation, I'd want to
> get this whole thing over as
> quickly and with as little
> pain as possible. So let's try
> our best to make this thing a
> simple in and out procedure.

Stan says nothing. Vinny comes over and puts his
hand on Stan's shoulder, massaging it, being
comforting. Stan's worst fears are confirmed.

> VINNY
>
> Maybe we should spend a
> coupla minutes to--get
> acquainted before we, you
> know, get to it.

Stan squirms away from Vinny, keeping his back to
the wall. He can't look Vinny in the eye.

> VINNY
>
> Whatsa matter?

> STAN
>
> I don't want to do this.

> VINNY
>
> I understand, but what're
> your alternatives?

> STAN
>
> My alternatives? To what? To
> you? I don't know . . .
>   (nervously)
> Suicide? Death?

> VINNY
>   (thinking it's a joke)
> That's it. It's either me . . .

```
                        (points to prison block)
                    . . . or them! You're gettin'
                    fucked one way or the other!²¹
```

The humor in this scene is based on Stan's innocence. He doesn't understand that Vinny (Joe Pesci) is Bill's cousin—their lawyer. The whole scene could be played perfectly straight; that's what makes it so funny.

One of the classically funny scenes of all time again uses context for its humor. In the conclusion of Billy Wilder's *Some Like It Hot*, Jerry (Jack Lemmon) and Osgood (Joe E. Brown) are riding in a speedboat. Osgood is dreamily happy, ignorant that Jerry is really a man in drag. Jerry maintains the charade in a blonde wig and falsetto voice.

```
                            OSGOOD
                    I called Mama--she was so
                    happy she cried--she wants
                    you to have her wedding gown
                    --it's white lace.

                            JERRY
                        (steeling himself)
                    Osgood--I can't get married
                    in your mother's dress. She
                    and I--we're not built the
                    same way.

                            OSGOOD
                    We can have it altered.

                            JERRY
                        (firmly)
                    Oh, no you don't. Look,
                    Osgood--I'm going to level
                    with you. We can't get
                    married at all.

                            OSGOOD
                    Why not?

                            JERRY
                    Well, to begin with, I'm not
                    a natural blonde.

                            OSGOOD
                        (tolerantly)
                    It doesn't matter.
```

                    JERRY
          And I smoke. I smoke all the
          time.

                    OSGOOD
          I don't care.

                    JERRY
          And I have a terrible past.
          For three years now, I've
          been living with a saxophone
          player.

                    OSGOOD
          I forgive you.

                    JERRY
            (with growing desperation)
          And I can never have
          children.

                    OSGOOD
          We'll adopt some.

                    JERRY
          But you don't understand!
            (he rips off his wig; in a
            male voice)
          I'm a MAN!

                    OSGOOD
            (oblivious)
          Well—nobody's perfect.[22]

The humor of this scene is heightened by the context—the audience knows all along that Jerry is a man. The joke is ultimately played not just on Jerry but on the audience as well.

Audience knowledge and expectations play a large role in the overall context of the dialogue. In the following scene from Todd Solondz's disturbing film, *Happiness*, the context creates remarkable tension. Bill Maplewood (Dylan Baker) is a successful psychiatrist with a secret—he's a pedophile. The audience knows this about Bill but the other characters don't. What could be an innocent scene takes on a much darker tone when Bill has an informal talk with his son, Billy (Rufus Read).

Billy sits beside Bill on the coach.

                    BILLY
          Dad?

                         BILL
           Yes, Billy?

                         BILLY
           I was kind of wondering.

                         BILL
           Yes.

Pause.

                         BILLY
           Nothing.

Pause.

                         BILL
           Did you have fun with Johnny?

                         BILLY
           Yeah . . . It was okay. He's a
           little girlish, though.

                         BILL
           Oh. Yeah.

Pause.

                         BILLY
           Dad, do you know how many
           inches your penis is?

Pause.

                         BILL
           I never measured.

                         BILLY
           'Cause Ronald Farber said his
           penis is eleven inches long.
           Do you think that's possible?

                         BILL
           What Ronald Farber doesn't
           know is that it's not length
           that matters; it's width.

Pause.

                         BILLY
           Why?

                         BILL
           Things get a little more . . .
           intense.

                        BILLY
            What do you mean . . . intense?

Pause.

                        BILL
            Have you been . . . practicing?

                        BILLY
            . . . Yeah. But it's no use.
            Nothing comes.

                        BILL
            You have to be patient. Your
            friend Ronald Farber, I can
            assure you, is full of crap.

                        BILLY
            Yeah. I bet yours is a lot
            wider and longer.

Pause.

                        BILL
            Do you want me to measure?

                        BILLY
            Nah, that's okay.

Billy smiles.[23]

The tension achieved through the context really works.

   Are there others ways to create tension or humor? Good question. Why not try a little experimentation?

EXPERIMENTAL DIALOGUE

Though there doesn't seem to be much experimentation with dialogue, occasionally a writer plays with language enough to push the edges of the narrative form creating experimental dialogue. One of the most provocative uses of experimental dialogue is found in Hal Hartley's film, *The Unbelievable Truth*. In this particular scene, Josh (Robert Burke) has just had a frustrating conversation with Audrey (Adrienne Shelly). After Audrey leaves, Josh sits and reads at a table in the café. A new Girl (Mary Sue Flynn) with very definite ideas, approaches Josh and tries to draw him into another conversation.

                        GIRL
            I know what you need.

                        JOSH
            Excuse me?

                    GIRL
You need a woman.

                    JOSH
Oh.

                    GIRL
That girl's crazy.

                    JOSH
I know but I like her.

                    GIRL
Yeah, but she's leaving town.

                    JOSH
So I've heard.

                    GIRL
So come on, what d'ya say? I
know what you need.

                    JOSH
Excuse me?

                    GIRL
You need a woman.

                    JOSH
Oh.

                    GIRL
That girl's crazy.

                    JOSH
I know but I like her.

                    GIRL
Yeah, but she's leaving town.

                    JOSH
So I've heard.

                    GIRL
So come on, what d'ya say? I
know what you need.

                    JOSH
Excuse me?

                    GIRL
You need a woman.

```
                JOSH
Oh.

                GIRL
That girl's crazy.

                JOSH
I know but I like her.

                GIRL
Yeah but she's leaving town.

                JOSH
So I've heard.

                GIRL
So come on, what d'ya say? I
know what you need.

                JOSH
Excuse me?

                GIRL
You need a woman.

                JOSH
Oh.

                GIRL
That girl's crazy.²⁴
```

The dialogue ends there and the next shot depicts Audrey walking down the street. Did you notice how the language takes on a circular pattern? What do you think Hartley was trying to accomplish by repeating some of the dialogue? Once you hear the dialogue within the context of the film, you may have a better sense of whether the experimental dialogue works or not.

Experimental dialogue is valuable because it forces you to think beyond convention. Writing should always involve playfulness and invention. With every subsequent draft of your script, you should be thinking about how to insure that your work is as original as it can be.

The following scene from *Galaxy Quest* was different in earlier drafts of the script. The playful aspects of the dialogue were enhanced in this version. The story is about a group of actors mistaken for their characters on a Trek-like, cancelled TV show, who are abducted by aliens. Known as Thermians, the aliens are a naïve, pacifist lot who believe the TV reruns of *Galaxy Quest* are documentaries and that the actors are members of a real spaceship crew. In this scene, the TV actors/crew have landed their pod

on an alien planet in search of a beryllium sphere. Gwen (Sigourney Weaver), Alexander (Alan Rickman), and Fred (Tony Shalhoub) hide behind boulders, observing small creatures mining an indeterminate substance. The playful language introduced in this draft of the script centers around a **pun** (play on words).

```
Suddenly they become aware of a SMALL BLUE CREATURE
emerging from one of the structures. It's blue and
looks somewhat like a human child. It moves to a
small pool of water and begins drinking.

Its movements are very quiet and tentative. Then a
few more BLUE CHILDREN emerge and join the first.
                    GWEN
               (smiling, amazed)
          Look at that . . . Will you
          LOOK at that . . . They look
          like little children . . .

                  ALEXANDER
          Could they be the miners?

                    FRED
          Sure. They're like, three
          years old.

                  ALEXANDER
          MINERS, not MINORS.

He pronounces the two words exactly the same. Fred
looks at Alex like he's crazy.25
```

Did the models inspire you? If so, you're probably itching to write your own dialogue.

Think of the characters you've created. How would you utilize dialogue to bring your characters to life? Would your characters use naturalistic or stylized dialogue, or both? Would your characters talk a lot or a little? If the audience could hear your characters' thoughts, what would they be thinking? Write a monologue for one of your characters. Now place your character in a different time period. Would the monologue change? Try placing your character in another part of the world. Does that change the monologue? Now write a scene with a few characters. Is it hard to write a scene without the context of the whole script?

How do the dynamics of the characters' respective personalities affect your scene?

A discussion of dialogue wouldn't be complete without considering the absence of dialogue—silence. Silence always has meaning. When one person abstains from participating in a conversation, silence may represent power, impotence, rage, sadness, or joy. Silence is capable of producing unrelenting tension or profound calm. Whatever the mood you want to evoke, silence is a powerful tool. If you use it wisely, it will enhance your dialogue and enrich your characters.

Now that you know what a script looks like, how to shape your story and bring your characters to life, you might want to think about trying to adapt a story from another source. A scriptwriter would be foolish to ignore the wealth of great stories that already exist. And, as always, there is much to be learned from the masters.

REFERENCES

1. Calder Willingham and Buck Henry, *The Graduate*, Avco Embassy Pictures, 1967.
2. Lily Tuck, *Interviewing Matisse or The Woman Who Died Standing Up*, Alfred A. Knopf, New York, 1991, p. 103.
3. Deborah Tannen, *You Just Don't Understand*, Ballantine Books, New York, 1990, pp. 174–175.
4. Ethan Coen and Joel Coen, *Fargo*, Faber and Faber, London, 1996, pp. 53–55.
5. Billy Bob Thornton, *Sling Blade*, Miramax Books, New York, 1996, pp. 109–110.
6. Thornton, pp. 65–66.
7. Joel Coen and Ethan Coen, *Blood Simple*, St. Martin's Press, New York, 1988, pp. 6–9. (In the book, the script is not in script format. For the purposes of consistency, I've maintained script format.)
8. John Singleton, *Boyz in the Hood*, Columbia Tri-Star, 1992.
9. Allison Anders, *Gas—Food—Lodging*, Cineville, 1991.
10. Noel Langley, Florence Ryerson, and Edgar Allan Woolf, *The Wizard of Oz* (adapted from a story by Noel Langley based on the novel by L. Frank Baum), Metro-Goldwyn-Mayer, 1939.
11. Paddy Chayefsky, *Network*, Metro-Goldwyn-Mayer, 1976.
12. Alan Ball, *American Beauty: The Shooting Script*, Newmarket Press, New York, 1999, p. 60.
13. Marc Norman and Tom Stoppard, *Shakespeare in Love*, Hyperion/Miramax Books, New York, 1998, pp. 9–11.
14. John Patrick Shanley, *Moonstruck*, Metro-Goldwyn-Mayer, 1987.

15. Jim Uhls, *Fight Club*, Fox 2000 Pictures, 1999.
16. Andrew Niccol, *The Truman Show: The Shooting Script*, Newmarket Press, New York, 1998, p. 64.
17. Woody Allen, *Hannah and Her Sisters*, Orion Pictures, 1986.
18. Nora Ephron, *When Harry Met Sally . . .* , Columbia, 1989.
19. William Goldman, *Butch Cassidy and the Sundance Kid*, 20th Century Fox, 1969.
20. Hilary Henkin and David Mamet, *Wag the Dog*, Tribeca Productions/New Line Cinema/Punch Productions/Baltimore Pictures, 1997.
21. Dale Launer (polish by Jonathan Lynn), *My Cousin Vinny*, 20th Century Fox, 1992.
22. Billy Wilder, *Some Like It Hot*, United Artists, Hollywood, 1959.
23. Todd Solondz, *Happiness*, Faber and Faber, 1998, pp. 52-53.
24. Hal Hartley, *The Unbelievable Truth*, Action Features/Miramax, 1990.
25. David Howard and Robert Gordon, *Galaxy Quest*, DreamWorks SKG, 1999.

Adaptation

—Norman Mailer

What do you think the following films have in common: *It Happened One Night, Gone with the Wind, Bridge on the River Kwai, A Man for All Seasons, In the Heat of the Night, Midnight Cowboy, The Godfather, One Flew Over the Cuckoo's Nest, Ordinary People, On Golden Pond, Terms of Endearment, Out of Africa, The Last Emperor, Dangerous Liaisons, Driving Miss Daisy, Dances with Wolves, Howard's End, Sense and Sensibility, Sling Blade, L.A. Confidential, Gods and Monsters, Silence of the Lambs, Schindler's List, Forrest Gump,* and *The Cider House Rules*? If your answer was that all these scripts (and respective scriptwriters, of course) won Oscars for Best Screenplays Based on Material from Another Medium, you're right.

If you had to guess how many Best Picture Oscars were adaptations, what would your guess be? According to the book *Adaptations from Text to Screen, Screen to Text,* "Eighty-five percent of all Academy Award-winning Best Pictures are adaptations. Forty-five percent of all TV movies-of-the-week are adaptations. Eighty-three percent of all TV mini-series are adaptations."[2]

Clearly, adaptations have a history of success. What this means in the context of your writing life is up to you. If you do decide to explore adaptation, you'll need to realign your thinking a bit, however.

Have you ever seen a film based on a book or other medium? What was your response? Did the scriptwriter effectively translate the original material to the screen? Listen to exit interviews at theatres—people usually have strong opinions about whether a work has been successfully adapted.

Writers are especially sensitive to seeing their own work brought to the silver screen. Among the literary greats who have seen, or contributed to, their works recreated as filmic stories are Tennessee Williams, John Steinbeck, Pearl Buck, William Faulkner, and Ernest Hemingway. The results have not always been satisfactory.

> Hollywood and writers have always made uneasy bedfellows. Ernest Hemingway never quite got over the movie based on his book, *The Snows of Kilimanjaro*. He always referred to it as "The Snows of Zanuck" and gave his own best-performer award to the hyena.[3]

Contemporary writers, too, have seen their works translated to both the large and small screens with varying degrees of satisfaction. Among the most frequently adapted contemporary writers are Michael Crichton, John Grisholm, Danielle Steele, Elmore Leonard, and Stephen King.

As you begin to adapt stories, you'll discover how difficult it is to write a visually compelling story that remains true to the spirit and integrity of the original work. Though adapting a work is a creative process similar to that of writing an original work, the decisions you will be faced with are quite unique. Not only will you want to select a work worthy of adaptation, you'll also need to solve new problems related specifically to the adaptive process.

Stanley Kramer, film director and producer, discusses the problems unique to adaptation in an interview in *Reel Conversations*.

> You can't be faithful. That's a ridiculous word in this instance. When a novelist sells a book, he sells it to people who read. When a writer adapts a novel, he has to sell it to a movie audience. He has to put it in film language which sometimes may be impossible to translate in visual terms. You hope that the spirit is true and remains solid, but he settles for an adaptation. Also, if you were to do it directly as a novel, you would have a four- or five-hour film, and unfortunately they're not in fashion. Distributors won't stand for that. No novelist is completely satisfied with the adaptation, because there've been cuts and you resent them—just as a filmmaker resents cuts which somebody else makes, and that's usually the distributor.[4]

Before you consider adapting a work, it helps to reinforce your knowledge of good storytelling. Read an abundance of original works to help develop your sensibilities. You should also read model stories and their respective script adaptations. This will give you the opportunity to examine the creative decisions made by professional scriptwriters in the process of adaptation. A terrific model to read would be Frank Darabont's adaptation of Stephen King's short story "Rita Hayworth and Shawshank Redemption" from King's short story collection *Different Seasons*. The adapted

script, including introductions by King and Darabont as well as sample storyboards and production notes, is available in *The Shawshank Redemption: The Shooting Script* from Newmarket Press. You might also want to read Darabont's more recent script, *The Green Mile*, based on King's serialized novel of the same name.

When you search for source material, don't overlook any source. A poem, short story, play, novel, news item, or true story may provide you with the makings of a story. To be worthy of adaptation, a story should also have the potential to be a strong visual story. Though an original work may be very powerful, if the story cannot be shown instead of told then it's probably not a good choice for adaptation. You may not feel confident enough to make that decision until you've written an adaptation. You'll have an opportunity to adapt a short story later in the chapter; in the meantime, the next writing prompt should help you begin to formulate questions about adaptation.

Think of your favorite fable or fairy tale. Why is that particular story a favorite? If you rewrote the story as a script, how would you reconceptualize it? What decisions would you have to make to rewrite the story? Maybe your choice would be a simple one, like changing the point of view. In his humorous book, *The True Story of the 3 Little Pigs*, Jon Scieszka (under the pseudonym A. Wolf) retells the story from the wolf's point of view. Seen through the wolf's eyes, the reader gains empathy for the wolf, who sees himself as a hapless victim.[5] Try rewriting the story you selected. How does your rewritten story differ from the original? Did you improve the story? Should you try to improve the story?

Fairy tales and fables are good sources since they're in the **public domain**. Any source material you find that's in the public domain is fair game for you to adapt. What is the public domain? When copyright protection ends for a creative work, unless the copyright is renewed, that work is considered to be in the public domain. When does copyright protection end for a creative work? Generally, copyrighted works created before 1978 (when there was a change in copyright law), remain copyrighted for a total of seventy-five years thereafter. Works created after 1978 are protected by copyright for the creator and his or her heirs for the lifetime of the creator plus fifty years. This is a simplified summary of copyright law. If you plan to adapt something and you want to know for certain whether it's in the public domain, contact the copyright office (see the Resources section for specific information) for details. If you do decide to adapt a work in the public domain, you'll be in good company. Films such as *West Side Story*,

Romeo and Juliet, *My Fair Lady*, *Hamlet*, *In the Company of Wolves*, *A Room with a View*, *Sense and Sensibility*, *The Age of Innocence*, *Clueless*, and *Titus* are among the abundant adaptations of work in the public domain.

OBTAINING RIGHTS

If you select source material that's not in the public domain, you'll need to obtain the rights to the work (unless you're adapting one of your own works to which you hold the copyright). To adapt a work without first receiving written permission to do so would be a waste of your time and talent.

If the original work is published, check the copyright page to find out who holds the copyright. Don't assume that the author owns the copyright. Scriptwriters usually relinquish their copyright to the studio or production company. Writers of poetry, nonfiction, or fiction may have abdicated partial or full rights to the publisher. If a publisher or studio owns the copyright, someone within the company will direct you to the appropriate contact person. Be prepared to establish yourself as a professional, justify your desire to adapt the work, and, in some cases, pay a substantial sum of money for the rights.

If the author is the copyright owner, the publisher may be able to tell you how to reach that person. If the author has an agent, the publisher will direct you to him or her. If the agent chooses not to cooperate with you in providing access to the author, you must then decide if you want to abandon the search or try to reach the author directly.

Finding the author is easier now that the World Wide Web is available. Oftentimes, authors will provide websites or email addresses with their books. If the author retains copyright, you may be able to email the author directly. If you can't reach the author by email, try snail mail. If you know where the author lives, you might write a letter. If you can't locate the author, you might consult a website for the Writers Guild or Poets & Writers (see the Resources section for specific addresses). If the author is deceased, see if the publisher or agent can provide you with the name of the lawyer who handled the estate.

You may find you'll have to dig even deeper. Library sources, personal journals, or periodicals pertinent to the life of the author may provide leads. Be patient. It almost always takes longer than you anticipate it will to find who owns the copyright for a work. Whatever the method you devise in contacting the copyright owner, make sure you project a professional persona. When you write or speak to someone regarding the original work, explain your goals clearly. Be sure you know exactly what you want and be ready to articulate your needs prior to contacting anyone. Also, don't forget to provide an address and phone number where you may be reached.

Once you've made contact with the copyright owner, you need to obtain written permission from the owner before you can adapt the work. You have no legal right to adapt a work without written permission unless the work is in the public domain.

At this time, you'll need to obtain a letter of agreement, or an option agreement. An **option agreement** enables you to have exclusive access to the copyrighted property for a period of time agreed upon by all parties. You will probably need to pay for an option. The cost of an option could range from one dollar to thousands of dollars. The amount will be determined by the value of the property, the willingness of the copyright owner to share the work with you, and your ability to negotiate. Before entering into an option agreement, you should consult a lawyer. If that's cost-prohibitive for you, and the copyright owner is willing to option the work for a small amount of money, there are standard forms that you may reproduce available in screenwriting books pertaining to the legal aspects of the business (refer to the Resources section for more information). Obviously, it's advisable to consult a lawyer to protect your interests. Though any respected lawyer will be able to help you negotiate with the copyright owner, you may want to contact a specialist in the field of entertainment law. An entertainment lawyer will be able to advise you about aspects of the law germane to entertainment. Though legal fees are expensive, you will save yourself money and hardship in the long run if you protect yourself before you begin to write.

You'll probably have more luck obtaining the rights to a short story in an obscure magazine than you will obtaining the rights to a novel. Forget best sellers—they get snatched up by Hollywood in the prepublication or galley stage. Keep in mind that the more obscure the original work, the better your chances are of obtaining the rights to the work.

You may be able to obtain rights to a true story that happened to someone you know or that you read about in a newspaper or magazine. Again, you will need to go directly to the source of the story to obtain permission. You'll also need to check to see if the subject of the story owns the rights. Sometimes subjects sell the rights to their own stories to help pay for living or legal expenses.

If you're interested in writing a true story as a movie-of-the-week, producers may be interested in your script if they think the story is hot. Just remember, tell a good story that you care about. Don't write a story solely because you think some producer might want to buy it.

THE ADAPTIVE PROCESS

Before beginning the process of adaptation, you'll need to know your source material thoroughly. If it's a true story, you'll want to research a

variety of sources, keeping scrupulous notes as you proceed. If your original work is fictitious, you'll need to reread the source as often as is necessary to focus on the heart of the work and to familiarize yourself with the story and characters. Again, diligent note-taking will solidify your work and will help you solve problems as you progress.

As you begin to envision the story as a script, remember your responsibility to show rather than tell the story. One of the challenges of adaptation is to reveal the interior lives of the characters through action. When you read a work of fiction, you often know the thoughts of the characters. Is it possible to show the thoughts of a character? If so, how? If not, how do you reveal the internal workings of the character?

Oftentimes scriptwriters elect to transmit the interior thoughts of the main character through a narrator's voice-over. Though this may work, too often this is an ineffective solution. Voice-overs should be used sparingly and with deliberate intent. If you choose this solution, it should only be after you've explored all means of telling the story visually. Avoid using a voice-over as a quick fix. Your ability to successfully adapt a work will depend upon the questions you ask yourself as you read and reread the original work.

To help you get started, you may want to consider the following questions:

- Can the story be told visually?
- From what or whose point of view should the story be told?
- Should the structure replicate the source material or does it need a newly conceived structure?
- Where does the story take place and who are the main characters? Are all the characters and locations necessary? If not, who or what should be omitted?
- Are there other elements of the source material that should not be incorporated into the new work?
- What strategies can you devise to solve the problem of omitting material without losing the intended meaning and spirit of the original work?

These questions and those you formulate during the adaptive process will guide you.

ADAPTATION IN ACTION

Now that you have a rudimentary understanding of adaptation, why not give it a try? The following very short story, "The Bank Robbery," by Steven Schutzman, should challenge you. Don't be deceived by the brevity

of the story; it's dense in meaning. Remember to apply your knowledge of script format as you write.

The bank robber told his story in little notes to the bank teller. He held the pistol in one hand and gave her the notes with the other. The first note said:

This is a bank holdup because money is just like time and I need more to keep on going, so keep your hands where I can see them and don't go pressing any alarm buttons or I'll blow your head off.

The teller, a young woman of about twenty-five, felt the lights that lined her streets go on for the first time in years. She kept her hands where he could see them and didn't press any alarm buttons. Ah danger, she said to herself, you are just like love. After she read the note, she gave it back to the gunman and said:

"This note is far too abstract. I really can't respond to it."

The robber, a young man of about twenty-five, felt the electricity of his thoughts in his hand as he wrote the next note. Ah money, he said to himself, you are just like love. His next note said:

This is a bank holdup because there is only one clear rule around here and that is WHEN YOU RUN OUT OF MONEY YOU SUFFER, *so keep your hands where I can see them and don't go pressing any alarm buttons or I'll blow your head off.*

The young woman took the note, touching lightly the gunless hand that had written it. The touch of

the gunman's hand went immediately to her memory, growing its own life there. It became a constant light toward which she could move when she was lost. She felt that she could see everything clearly as if an unknown veil had just been lifted.

"I think I understand better now," she said to the thief, looking first in his eyes and then at the gun. "But all this money will not get you what you want." She looked at him deeply, hoping that she was becoming rich before his eyes.

Ah danger, she said to herself, you are the gold that wants to spend my life.

The robber was becoming sleepy. In the gun was the weight of his dreams about this moment when it was yet to come. The gun was like the heavy eyelids of someone who wants to sleep but is not allowed.

Ah money, he said to himself, I find little bits of you leading to more of you in greater little bits. You are promising endless amounts of yourself but others are coming. They are threatening our treasure together. I cannot pick you up fast enough as you lead into the great, huge quiet that you are. Oh money, please save me, for you are desire, pure desire, that wants only itself.

The gunman could feel his intervals, the spaces in himself, piling up so that he could not be sure of what he would do next. He began to write. His next note said:

Now is the film of my life, the film of my insomnia: an eerie bus ride, a trance in the night, from which I

want to step down, whose light keeps me from sleeping.
In the streets I will chase the wind-blown letter of
love that will change my life. Give me the money, my
Sister, so that I can run my hands through its hair.
This is the unfired gun of time, so keep your hands
where I can see them and don't go pressing any alarm
buttons or I'll blow your head off with it.

Reading, the young woman felt her inner hands grabbing and holding onto this moment of her life.

Ah danger, she said to herself, you are yourself with perfect clarity. Under your lens I know what I want.

The young man and woman stared into each other's eyes forming two paths between them. On one path his life, like little people, walked into her, and on the other hers walked into him.

"This money is love," she said to him. "I'll do what you want." She began to put money into the huge satchel he had provided.

As she emptied it of money, the bank filled with sleep. Everyone else in the bank slept the untroubled sleep of trees that would never be money. Finally she placed all the money in the bag.

The bank robber and the bank teller left together like hostages of each other. Though it was no longer necessary, he kept the gun on her, for it was becoming like a child between them.[6]

Now that you've had the opportunity to adapt a story, think about the process you went through. Did you find the story appropriate for adaptation? If not, why not? What specific problems did you encounter as you

wrote your adaptation? What inevitably gets lost during adaptation? What questions did you have to ask yourself? What did you learn about the process of adaptation?

The following script is my adaptation of the story. You may want to read it to see how it differs from yours. Obviously, there are myriad possibilities for adapting the story.

```
FADE IN:

EXT. BANK - MORNING

Tarnished letters reading "Trust Savings" adorn a
skinny, stone-faced building sandwiched between Bud's
Used Appliances and an abandoned storefront.

INT. BANK

Chipped tile floors, musty leather furniture, worn
paneling. Neglect reigns. Several CUSTOMERS patiently
wait in line for the only teller.

The TELLER, a pallid-faced woman in her mid-twenties,
mechanically snaps the band from a stack of tens.
Without looking up, she deals out the crisp tens like
a Vegas dealer to a blue-haired, elderly WOMAN.

                    TELLER
          That's ten, twenty, and
          thirty.

The Woman takes her money and leaves.

                    TELLER
          Next.

A ROBBER steps up to the counter. Twenty-five, looks
younger. T-shirt. Jeans. Unshaven. Wild hair and
eyes. Looks like he just rolled out of bed.

He slides a note under the bars to the Teller. The
Teller quickly surveys the note. Looks up at the
man. He's pointing a pistol directly at her heart.

                    TELLER
          This note is far too
          abstract. I really can't
          respond to it.

She slips her hand beneath the bars and shows him
the note.
```

> TELLER
> See this part. "Money is just
> like time and I need more to
> keep on going." It's too
> vague. Do you need more money
> or more time?

The Robber leans in closer to the Teller.

> ROBBER
> See this part. "Don't go
> pressing any alarm buttons
> or I'll blow your head off."
> Is that specific enough
> for you?

The Teller's face flushes. She returns the note to him, purposefully touching his hand.

> TELLER
> Try again.

The Robber flips the note over and scribbles furiously on the back of it. He hands it over to her. As she reads the note, the customers behind the Robber grow sleepy, rubbing their eyes and yawning.

> TELLER
> Fifty thousand dollars.
> That's much better. But this
> new part, "when you run out
> of money you suffer," doesn't
> work for me.

The Teller slides the note back to him, her hand lingering on his as they touch, her eyes burning with desire.

> TELLER
> I think I understand better
> now. But all this money won't
> get you what you want.

Moving slowly, dreamily, the Robber takes the note back from her, crosses out the original note, and begins writing in bold, deliberate strokes. Each stroke of the pen arouses the Teller. As he writes, the customers slump to the floor and fall asleep.

The Robber hands the newly penned note to the
Teller. He watches her eyes as she reads. A strand
of hair falls in her face. The Robber reaches his
hand through the bars and softly moves the hair back
into place. She looks up to meet the Robber's gaze.

Suddenly, she grabs stacks and stacks of money and
shoves them into a bag.

                    TELLER
            This money is love. I'll do
            what you want.

Effortlessly, the Teller slings the bag of money
over her back. Struts out from behind the counter.
The Robber takes her hand, keeping the gun on her.
She leans into him, kissing him hungrily, cradling
the gun between them gently as a child.

In earlier drafts of the script, I took a more realistic stance, showing impatient, disgruntled customers in the teller's line. But I decided that I didn't like the loss of the dreamlike, fairytale quality of the story, so I rewrote the actions of the customers to more closely resemble the story.

Did you show the audience what was in the Robber's notes? My first inclination was to reveal the text of the notes verbatim, but I liked the idea of their contents being more mysterious. It also heightened the intimacy of the central characters, intentionally leaving us on the outside.

I share my conceptual chain of thoughts with you so that you may understand that there is no single, right interpretation and that part of the process is making decisions that support your concept of what needs to happen in the story. As you approach longer works, you'll probably have to look more closely at what should be included and excluded without betraying the intent of the original work.

As a scriptwriter, you have to make decisions. When you're working on an adaptation, your decisions will reflect your desire to be true to the intent of the original work. What other decisions do you anticipate having to make as a scriptwriter?

The decisions you make should not only be concerned with what stories to tell, but also how those stories might influence your audience. This raises the ethical question: do you, as a scriptwriter, have any responsibility toward your audience? The question is significant enough to be the center of thought in the next chapter.

REFERENCES

1. Tony Crawley, ed., *Chambers Film Quotes*, W & R Chambers Ltd, Edinburgh, 1991. From a quote by Norman Mailer first cited in *Deauville*, September 6, 1982.
2. Deborah Cartmell and Imelda Watlehan, *Adaptations from Text to Screen, Screen to Text*, Routledge, London, 1999, p. 3.
3. James Charlton and Lisbeth Mark, *The Writer's Home Companion*, Penguin Books, New York, 1987, p. 63.
4. George Hickenlooper, ed., *Reel Conversations: Candid Interviews with Film's Foremost Directors and Critics*, Carol Publishing Group, New York, 1991, p. 155. From an interview with Stanley Kramer.
5. Jon Scieszka, *The True Story of the 3 Little Pigs*, Viking Kestrel, New York, 1989.
6. Steven Schutzman, "The Bank Robbery" originally published in *Sudden Fiction*, Peregrine Smith Books, Salt Lake City, 1986, pp. 94–95.

The Abuses of Enchantment

Messages are for Western Union.[1]

—Samuel Goldwyn

Samuel Goldwyn was a movie mogul who believed, as many people do, that movies are strictly for entertaining people and making money. Goldwyn felt that movies shouldn't be concerned with sending messages to the audience; that job should be left to parents, churches, and schools. Whether you share Goldwyn's viewpoint or not, the reality is, intentionally or unintentionally, movies do send messages.

If you doubt the power of the messages sent by the filmic medium, you might heed the actions and words of the young. After dropping acid with her seventeen-year-old boyfriend, an eighteen-year-old girl repeatedly watched *Natural Born Killers*, then (emulating the behavior of the film's characters) killed one person and left another paralyzed. That girl is now serving a thirty-five-year sentence for armed robbery and attempted second-degree murder in the Louisiana Correctional Institute for Women.[2] (Ironically, both teenagers missed Stone's underlying anti-violent message, revealed subtextually through the film's stylistic indictment of the mainstream media's obsession with violence.)

Unfortunately, this media-influenced incident is not an isolated story. On April 20, 1999, two high school students clad in Matrix-like, black leather trenchcoats went on a killing spree at Columbine High School. As investigators unraveled the boys' respective pasts, they discovered disturbing revelations from websites, journals, and secret videos left by the boys. Not only were the boys' actions influenced by films (they specifically cited

261

Reservoir Dogs as well as a variety of gory videogames), the boys also made it clear that they wanted movies made of their story. They surmised that directors would fight over their story and they argued over who could be trusted with the script—Steven Spielberg or Quentin Tarantino.[3] (You may have noticed that I omitted the names of the teenagers. This was a purposeful act, an attempt to sabotage the will of the boys' hunger for fame as well as the media's contribution to their infamy.)

Media influences on the behavior and attitudes of children begin at an early age. When elementary school students from Dixie Canyon Elementary School in Los Angeles were interviewed as part of the Writers Guild's Literacy Project, the results revealed that images do affect how young people think about violence, race, gender, and economics. In the following segments of the interview, some of the students share their views.

On Violence

Lindsay Rosenthal: I mean, there's a lot of violence in the world today, but there's also a lot of nice things. People focus on what's violent instead of what's good. Then they build off that and make it worse and worse instead of better and better.

Richard Gonzalez: I was thinking the same thing—that it isn't right to show people going out into the street and killing people for nothing all the time.

On Race

Krista Fisher: A lot of movies show blacks as bad.

Lindsay Marks: They do that to make money. They don't really care. Well they care as long as it's 'good,' but they don't really care if it's prejudiced.

On Gender

Lindsay R: Like *Indecent Proposal*, a guy spends a million dollars to have a night with Demi Moore. That's like saying Demi Moore is a hooker, since she is pretty every guy would want her, and money can get you what you want.

Lindsay M: If I had my choice, I'd be a boy. In movies and TV shows the guy gets to do more stuff. Also in real life.

On Economics

Lindsay M: The houses and things they show on TV aren't like real life. Mansions and stuff. We should be happy with what we have and shouldn't be worrying about what we don't have.

Krista: But it makes you think, why is this on TV? Why isn't it in real life? Why can't I have that house?[4]

The thoughtful responses of these children affirm that though it may not be the intent of the filmmaker to send messages, movies impart cultural messages nonetheless.

Does this mean that you should censor yourself as you write, that you should create only politically correct stories and characters? Absolutely not. Censorship is not the answer, nor is pasteurizing your characters into a bland but safe oneness that does not reflect the culture at large.

It does mean that you should begin asking questions of yourself about the role visual stories play within the context of our culture and within a larger historical context.

Think of the films you saw as a child. Did any of them frighten you so much that the images have haunted you throughout the years? Were there any films that prompted you to go out and behave as the characters? As an adult, have any of your ideas about love and marriage been influenced by the movies? What expectations about romance are created by the movies you see? About gender? Think of how the movies have romanticized other subjects—war, for instance. Were you ever involved in a war? If so, have you ever seen a movie that romanticized and trivialized war? Have you ever seen a film that accurately depicted war? Do you think the stories told in films have more of an influence on you than those you read in books? If so, why?

THE ABUSES OF ENCHANTMENT

Within this historical horizon, scriptwriters fulfill the function once assumed by oral storytellers. Storytelling was once relegated to tribal leaders, and later families assumed the roles of cultural storytellers. With the breakdown of tribal and family structures, visual storytelling has emerged as the dominant mode of relaying stories. Narrative scriptwriters have become what could be likened to postmodern Homers in a global village. Scriptwriters are the Shapers, the storytellers who are able to still the heart and ignite the mind. What responsibility, if any, does the storyteller bear toward the audience? In order to answer that, it might be helpful to examine the cultural significance of storytelling. In her book *Touch Magic*, Jane Yolen elaborates.

> Storytelling is our oldest form of remembering the promises we have made to one another and to our various gods, and the promises given in return; it is a way of recording our human emotions and desires and taboos. Whoever dares tell a story must bear in mind that the story is an essential part of our humanness.[5]

Since the advent of storytelling, stories have entertained humankind. Yet even the simplest stories impart the morals and myths of a culture.

Aesop's fables are didactic stories concluded by short maxims to help the child remember the lesson of the story. In *The Uses of Enchantment: The Meaning and Importance of Fairy Tales*, Bruno Bettelheim suggests that fairy tales represent symbolic solutions to existential problems.

> For example, in discussing 'Hansel and Gretel,' the child's striving to hold on to his parents even though the time has come for meeting the world on his own is stressed, as well as the need to transcend a primitive orality, symbolized by the children's infatuation with the gingerbread house. Thus, it would seem that this fairy story has most to offer to the young child ready to make his first steps out into the world. It gives body to his anxieties, and offers reassurance about these fears because even in their most exaggerated form—anxieties about being devoured—they prove unwarranted: the children are victorious in the end, and a most threatening enemy—the witch—is utterly defeated.[6]

In his persuasive work, Bettelheim stresses the positive aspects of enchantment. Yet an examination of the word "enchantment" reveals a pejorative etymology. "Enchantment" is a derivative of "enchant" from the Latin *incantare*, meaning "to chant, as in magic words." Its contemporary usage is "to cast under a spell; bewitch." An implied wickedness is inherent in the words "spell" and "bewitched." Fairy godmothers bestow wishes; witches cast spells.

The use or abuse of enchantment is dependent upon the storyteller and the medium in which the story is told. Oral storytelling, even when supported by visual gestures, requires that the listener abstract meaning from spoken language. The reader of lexical texts abstracts meaning from written language. In each instance, the participants understand that the story is fiction.

The media of film and television introduce a perplexing problem for the viewer. Since visual imagery is concrete rather than abstract, the viewer's interaction is inherently different from that of the listener's or reader's. Though the viewer may be cognitively aware that a film is fiction, the photographic properties of the medium create the illusion of reality. The verisimilitude of the cinematic image is supported by its symbiotic relationship with the still photographic image, especially as a credible source of truth as in the historical parallels of the newsreel and journalistic photograph. As Noel Carroll asserts:

> So there is, at the very least, a strong historic bond between cinematography and verisimilitude which, for contemporary film theorists, also involves a bond with illusionism. Thus, the photographic nature of the cinematic image is of key concern for contemporary film theorists who attempt to isolate the ways in which the photographic aspect of the cinematic image contributes to the production of ideology.[7]

This confusion between reality and illusion, between fact and fiction, makes the contemporary viewer vulnerable. Though narrative, visual stories may appear to be real, they are fictional. This is compounded by the fact that screen fictions are, like oral stories, value laden. Michael Parenti elaborates:

> Today, very little of our make-believe is drawn from children's games, storytelling, folktales, and fables, very little from dramas and dreams of our own making. Instead we have the multibillion-dollar industries of Hollywood and television to fill our minds with prefabricated images and themes.[8]

Along with manufactured images and themes come manufactured needs. The creation of artificial needs drives our economy. As we become increasingly dependent upon technology, we begin to believe that technology is something we need to survive rather than a tool created to serve us.

The blurring of reality and fantasy is further compounded as technological advancements create even more seductive virtual realities. The gaming industry, for one, is developing games that are becoming increasingly realistic. In her book, *Hamlet on the Holodeck*, Janet Murray describes immersive cyberspace gaming experiences.

> In digital environments we can put on a mask by acting through an avatar. An avatar is a graphical figure like a character in a videogame. In many Internet games and chat rooms, participants select an avatar in order to enter the common space. Even when avatars are crudely drawn or offer a very limited choice of personalization, they can still provide alternate identities than can be energetically employed. For instance, the inclusion of graphic avatars in the networked action game called *Quake* led players to organize themselves into clans. Each clan dresses its avatars in the same colors, and its members fight together against other clans. *Quake* players have created an array of clan web pages, which look like what the Crips and Bloods might create if they traded semiautomatics for laptop computers.[9]

Imagine how detrimental an immersive game of this nature might be to an alienated child who has difficulty discriminating between fact and fiction. What cultural guidelines do we provide children to discriminate between real and imaginary worlds? Are there any assurances that with the advancement of technology, developers will not exploit the cyberworld in the same way that they have the film industry?

Audiences are not interacting with benign entertainments; big business is bewitching them. For the scriptwriter, this presents a genuine ethical and artistic dilemma.

BEWITCHED, BOTHERED, AND BEWILDERED

The European film director Kryzysztof Zanussi said, "In Polish there is no semantic equivalent for the term "film business." The words are incongruent because film is art and business is business."[10] Filmmaking in America is sometimes about art; it is always about business.

> According to *Variety*'s 1999 Year in Review, the total for domestic movie ticket sales was 7.3 billion dollars, a 9 percent increase from 1998 (excluding ancillary markets such as video and foreign sales). Predictions run high for the future, too, as high as 7 to 9 percent every year.[11]

Business appears to be good.

Any good businessperson knows that business is based on demand for product. Yet the film industry has been historically mystified by what that demand is and what that product should be. Groping for an answer, the industry has inadvertently created an unwritten but widely accepted model for successful films, which looks something like this:

FORMULAIC SCRIPT + ELEMENTS = $

Formulaic scripts are those that follow a predictable pattern and feature stereotypical characters. **Elements** are powerful people such as bankable actors, actresses, and directors who could be part of an overall production "**package**." Combined, they create what the industry believes is a money-generating product.

The studios justify this mentality by selective recognition; that is, they enumerate the successes of blockbuster movies that follow the equation and treat the box office failures as isolated quirks of the system. Peter Biskind exemplifies this justification.

> When a *Hudson Hawk* flops, the studios never conclude that audiences are tired of action movies but rather that this particular example was somehow flawed; when *City of Joy* flops, however, the reverse is true. It's not the flawed but the whole, and so no movies with serious intent will be made for the next decade. My guess is that when these films are good, people go. They went to *JFK* and *Boyz N the Hood*.[12]

Even films intended to relay thoughtful messages to the audience are often impeded by industry practices. The process of taking a script from its first draft to the final shooting script is often treated as a form of premeditated censorship by the studios.

A case in point is *Fatal Attraction*. James Dearden conceived of the idea for the script when his wife was out of town and he fantasized about calling a woman he had met at a party some six months earlier. In the original plot,

stated very simply, a man drops his wife and child at the station, picks up the phone, and calls this woman. They go to bed; later he regrets his improprieties. She calls him. He goes to see her but makes it clear that his actions were in error. In despair, she cuts her wrists. He returns home the next day and the girl calls again. This time the wife is home and she answers. The screen goes blank.[13] It was Dearden's intent ". . . to explore an individual's responsibility for a stranger's suffering: he wanted to examine how this man who inflicted pain, no matter how unintentionally, must eventually hold himself accountable."[14] Dearden's original story was a moral tale.

From this script, Dearden created a highly acclaimed, forty-five-minute film called *Diversion* that was shown at the Chicago Film Festival. The script came to the attention of Sherry Lansing and Stanley Jaffe, who together had formed an independent movie production company affiliated with a major studio.

Lansing liked the feminist dimension of the script, the fact that the man was forced to face the consequences of his actions. However, once the script was within the domain of the studio system, Dearden was encouraged to make changes to the story. With each rewrite, the husband became more likeable and the single woman more predatory. Susan Faludi's book, *Backlash: The Undeclared War Against American Women*, presents the case in far more detail, yet the point is clear: the studios took what was essentially a moral tale about the consequences of a man's transgressions and turned it into a condemnation of a single woman. The covert cultural messages are that single women are dangerous threats to the institution of marriage and that men should be forgiven their transgressions while women should be punished for theirs.

This intrusive, interventionist action by the studios is standard practice within the industry. The interaction between the studios and the writer is one of negotiating power rather than negotiating meaning. And without the ability to negotiate meaning, writers are rendered impotent—for the freedom to negotiate meaning is what empowers the writer and enlivens the creative act.

The industry operates according to the fallacy that the only function of writing is to create an end product—a marketable commodity. Even the terms alluding to scripts and the writing process reflect industrial thinking. A script is a **property** to be bought and sold like a slab of meat at the market.

Though it is the end product that rightly concerns the industry, it is the process that must concern you, the scriptwriter. Approximately 20,000 to 25,000 writers register their scripts with the Writers Guild every year, yet only a minute percentage of those scripts are ultimately produced as films.

Does that mean that all of the unpurchased, unproduced scripts are worthless? If you are unable to sell your script, does that mean that all of

your labor was a waste of time and effort? Never. If you've told a genuine story and pursued your craft in earnest, you never lose. For it is in the process that you learn your craft; it is in the process that you find your voice. Your voice is necessary because you are a storyteller in a culture where visual stories have a significant impact on the audience. Your voice has the power to help shape the collective consciousness.

No one should tell you what stories to tell. As Jack Valenti, CEO and president of the Motion Picture Arts Association, stated in response to the government's concern regarding media violence,

> No one needs to tell a storyteller when 'just enough' becomes 'too much.' . . . Nobody needs to instruct you or anybody else how to tell your story so you are sensitive to action that may not be necessary. It's your decision. It's your responsibility.[15]

Consciousness cannot be legislated. Yet as a writer you have the unique opportunity to implement change by educating your audience about humankind's inhumanity toward one another through characters and stories that leave the audience moved or provoked. You have the power to heal people's spirits through laughter. You have the power to pose the questions that need to be asked.

What happens to a culture in which no one poses questions or provokes new thought? When the philosophers, poets, and storytellers have lost their voices, who will ask the questions?

If any system destroys the collective voice of the storytellers, it represents a cultural loss that once lost, may never be regained. As the storyteller in Wim Wenders' film *Wings of Desire* asks:

> Should I now give up? If I do give up, mankind will lose its story-teller. And once mankind loses its story-teller, then it will have lost its childhood. . . . Where are my heroes? Where are you, my children? Where are my own, the dull-witted, the first, the original ones? Name me, muse, the immortal singer who, abandoned by his mortal listeners, lost his voice. How, from being the angel of story-telling, he became an organ-grinder, ignored and mocked, outside, on the threshold of no-man's land.[16]

Your voice should resound with the stories that come from deep within. Remember the power the teller of stories holds. You will be less likely to abuse your role as an enchanter if you understand the responsibility that you bear toward your audience and the culture at large.

Magic is a powerful elixir. Imagine that you've happened upon a magic lantern. You rub it and—surprise—a genie appears. The genie grants you three wishes for yourself. What will they be?

REFERENCES

1. Gary Herman, ed., *The Book of Hollywood Quotes*, Omnibus Press, London, 1979. p. 25.
2. Susan Schindehette and Michelle McCalope, "Once Upon a Time," *People*, December 20, 1999, p. 82.
3. Nancy Gibbs and Timothy Roche, "The Columbine Tapes," *Time*, December 20, 1999, pp. 42 and 44.
4. Editorial Board of the Writers Guild, "Kids Say the Darndest Things: Six L. A. Youths Look at the Entertainment Business," *The Journal*, July 1993, pp. 18–21.
5. Jane Yolen, *Touch Magic*, Philomel Books, New York, 1981, p. 25.
6. Bruno Bettelheim, *The Uses of Enchantment: The Meaning and Importance of Fairy Tales*, Vintage Books Edition, New York, 1989, p. 15.
7. Noel Carroll, *Mystifying Movies: Fads and Fallacies in Contemporary Film Theory*, Columbia University Press, New York, 1988, p. 107.
8. Michael Parenti, *Make-Believe Media: The Politics of Entertainment*, St. Martin's Press, New York, 1992, p. 1.
9. Janet Murray, *Hamlet on the Holodeck*: *The Future of Narrative in Cyberspace*, The MIT Press, Cambridge, 1999, p. 113.
10. Kryzysztof Zanussi, quoted from an informal lecture with the students of the University of Central Florida's film division in Orlando, Florida on September 28, 1991.
11. Variety.com, 1999 Year in Review, 2000.
12. Peter Biskind, "Mind Rot," *Premiere*, August 1992, p. 51. Biskind went on to say, "Movies have an enormous impact. They are not 'just entertainment,' and the people who make them have an opportunity—even a responsibility—to have a positive effect on American culture." I find that an especially significant commentary from *Premiere*, a publication reflecting the popular rather than the elite culture.
13. Susan Faludi, *Backlash: The Undeclared War Against American Women*, Crown Publisher, New York, 1991, pp. 117–123.
14. Faludi, p. 117.
15. Robert Marich, "Valenti: TV must bend on violence," *The Hollywood Reporter*, January 28–30, 1994, p. 69.
16. Wim Wenders with Peter Handke (additional script work by Richard Reitinger), *Wings of Desire*, Road Movies and Argos Films, 1988. Transcribed from the English subtitles.

$$11$$

A Personal POV

Yeah well, that's just, ya know, like, your opinion, man.

—The Dude (Jeff Bridges) responding to a challenge from Jesus
(John Turturro) at the bowling alley in *The Big Lebowski*[1]

As you approach the end of your journal, and the beginning of your journey as a scriptwriter, you should keep in mind that what I've shared with you is my personal point of view. Feel free to make a liar of me. I don't pretend to be an all-knowing guru of scriptwriting. I have no magic formulas. What I do have is a love of writing.

Writers are wordsmiths. A wordsmith is a worker whose materials are words. Great scriptwriters are wordsmiths who not only can tell a great story but who can do so with style. Style comprises those distinctive qualities of writing that reveal a writer's skill and uniqueness. Style is particularly difficult to attain in scriptwriting because script style utilizes language economically, allowing the writer fewer words and less room for breathing within the text.

You can't acquire style by making a conscious decision to write with style; style comes with dedication to writing as you produce a body of work. The more you write, the more your work will be refined and defined until a genuine style emerges.

A writer's style is often not recognized as a significant contribution to a film since film is a collaborative art and directors are often considered the *auteur* (French for author) of the film. Yet it's the writer's style, the writer's imprint on the work, which is both the impetus for the work and the guiding force of the work. Andrew Sarris, a respected film critic, elaborates.

When I watch a film I always look for screenwriting. I'm very conscious of where films come from. An unfortunate line or a brilliant line is a

crucial point with audiences, but they're not always aware of everything else. Movies are a collective art. However, that does not mean that everybody who contributes to building a cathedral is responsible for the design of it. I say that is bullshit. I mean, to be an interesting work, somebody's personality has to come to the fore so you have style. You have to find the human element in it. That's the point. That's what people find difficult to say, and they thought it was like teamwork. But narrative, dramatic art, isn't a question of teamwork. It's somebody's story, and it's somebody's feeling that comes through if it's any good.[2]

That personality, that feeling to which Sarris alludes, is the writer's voice resonating in the work.

So how does a writer develop a voice in a collaborative medium? With great difficulty. If you really want to stretch, test yourself, develop your voice as a writer, you may want to consider embracing other forms of writing in addition to scriptwriting.

Why do you think you write? If your answer is to express yourself, to articulate a vision, to develop a voice, then you should experiment with other forms of writing. Novelist Rita Mae Brown (*Rubyfruit Jungle*, *Venus Envy*, *Bingo*) advises scriptwriters in her book, *Starting from Scratch: A Different Kind of Writers' Manual*.

A work of literature must be the artistic expression of *one, unified consciousness*. A screenplay or teleplay is never that. It is a cooperative venture or, sometimes, an uncooperative venture. It may be genius. It is still not literature. Even if you are very good at screenplays and teleplays, if you want to push yourself to the limit, you've got to work part of the year or part of your life with novels, poetry, plays, or short stories.[3]

Novelist and scriptwriter Ruth Prawer Jhabvala (writer of over half of Merchant Ivory's forty-plus films, including *Howard's End*, *Mr. and Mrs. Bridge*, *Remains of the Day*, and *A Room with a View*) concurs. Ms. Jhabvala explains how, when you're writing a novel, you get to be everybody. "You're not just the writer: You are the director and the actors. You decide what everyone is going to wear, how they're going to say their lines, exactly where the camera is going to be looking. A screenplay is more of a blueprint that others fill out."[4]

There are pragmatic arguments for writing in other forms as well. Not only will you have a greater opportunity to develop your voice, you'll also increase the chances for your work to be disseminated. Consider this.

Approximately 55,000 new books are published each year. Only 300 to 400 movies are put into production, yet 20,000 new stories and screenplays are registered with the Writers Guild of America. Calculate the number of people writing books versus the number of people writing screenplays,

and you might get some idea of where the better odds are. Since many New York publishers will read manuscripts from unknown authors, but hardly anyone at a movie studio will read a new writer's screenplays except on the recommendation of a trusted friend, it shouldn't be hard to figure out your odds. Besides, if you sell your book, there's a chance that it might do well and you'll get more money for a paperback sale. If the movie rights sell, that's another check (unless it's published first in paperback). If there are ancillary rights, such as a video or computer game spinoff or a TV series, you have many more opportunities to make money off one property.[5]

Though money is certainly a necessity for surviving, having a voice is a necessity for being. If you have a point of view you want to express, if you want to move or disturb an audience, if you want to provoke someone to think long after the flickering on the screen subsides, you must have a voice.

What is a writer's voice and how do you know if you have a legitimate voice as a writer? In Nick Bantock's novel *The Forgetting Room*, Mrs. Basquers, an irritating woman "cemented in thick makeup," asks the main character, a bookbinder, about his voice.

"And do *you write*, Mr. Hurt?"
Before I could catch myself I responded, "No, Mrs. Basquers, I don't write—I'm too aware of the difference between writing for the sake of it and having something to say."
What pompous garbage I speak when I'm defensive.
I'd never tried to write, for the same reason I didn't paint, because I didn't have a clue what to say. To me nothing was ever substantial enough to be worth expressing.[6]

Clearly, Mr. Hurt understands his limitations and is honest with himself.

Are you honest with yourself? Do you know why you write? Do you have something to say to an audience? If you don't feel you have anything worth expressing, look to other wordsmiths for inspiration. Who are some of your favorite wordsmiths? Do you have a favorite scriptwriter, playwright, essayist, journalist, songwriter, novelist, or poet? What is it about that person's style that distinguishes the work? Do you have any lines memorized from a film, song, novel, poem, from anywhere? If so, why do you think those lines remain with you? What is it about those lines that speak to you? Have you ever tried writing anything else other than a script? If so, what were the results? What have you written of which you're most proud?

Once you're confident you have a story worth telling, a script worth sharing, what do you do next? Good question.

Before you circulate your finished script, make sure it's worthy. Worthiness is, of course, a judgment call, but there are some stable factors that apply to any good script.

Here are some questions you should ask yourself before you place your script in the hands of an agent or producer. Check those questions with "yes" answers.

- Have you told a great story?
- Do the first ten pages of the story hook the reader and thrust the story forward?
- Is your script peopled with complex characters?
- Does the structure support the conceptual spine of your story?
- Does your script reflect a developed style (flair, subtext, irony, etc.)?
- Are the themes in your story evident to the reader?
- Is this your calling-card script, the script that best represents you as a writer?
- Have you, and preferably someone else, proofread your script for typos and syntactic errors?
- Is your final draft polished and complete?
- Is your script presented in professional format and ready to be submitted according to industry standards?
- Is your script protected by copyright and/or registration?

If you can answer "yes" to all of these questions, then you're on your way. The questions may have even raised other questions for you. For instance, should you copyright or register your script?

COPYRIGHT AND REGISTRATION

Though you have no legal obligation to copyright or register your work, it is in your best interest to do so. As of 1989, copyright notice is no longer required. However, if you want to prove authorship in a court of law, establishing copyright is the best legal evidence supporting the originality of your work. To establish immediate copyright and the best legal protection for yourself, your title page should have (1) either the copyright symbol © (preferred because it suits the Universal Copyright Convention requirements), the word Copyright, or the abbreviation Copr.; (2) the year of completion or the first publication; and (3) the name of the copyright owner.[7] Once you have posted copyright on the cover page of your script, your work

is technically copyrighted. To assure the best legal protection, it's advisable to contact the United States Copyright Office and register your script with their office. The procedure to follow is included in the Resources section of this book.

The next most effective method of establishing authorship is by registering your script with the Writers Guild West or East. These are active guilds with paid memberships and extensive benefits for members. You need to have professional experience to become a member of the Guild but you don't have to be a member to register your script with them. Some writers register their work with both the Writers Guild and the copyright office, though it's not necessary to do both. It is important to establish some record of authorship.

Another option for establishing the originality and completion date of your work is through the mail. Sending a sealed script to yourself via registered mail is another form of establishing a record of authorship. Though this method is the least expensive, it's legally unsound. You'd be wise to spend the extra money up front and copyright or register your work.

Once you've registered your work, you'll need to get your work to someone within the industry who can help you get your script produced. If you're lucky enough to have a relative or friend in the business, don't hesitate to ask that person to read your script or pass it on to an appropriate person. There's no stigma associated with nepotism in the film business.

AGENTS, LAWYERS, AND MANAGERS

As you begin to circulate your script, you should try to get it to an agent. Though it's difficult to get agents to read your work, it's not impossible. If you're lucky enough to get a reputable agent who wants to represent you, be thankful. Though you will have to pay the agent a percentage of your payment, you're much more likely to sell your script if an accomplished agent is peddling it. And remember, 10 percent of nothing is nothing.

You should always check to make sure that the agency is reputable. If they request a reader's fee, it's probably a scam. For a nominal fee, the Writers Guild will send you a list of approved agents. Be sure when you read through the list that you check to see which agencies will accept **unsolicited scripts**; that is, those that are not requested. Don't bother to send your script to an agency that has already stated that they won't take unsolicited scripts.

The large, established agencies are power players who are well connected within the industry and have the best chance of selling your script. The only problem with the powerful agencies is that they will work hardest for their established, money-making clients, and unless they consider your

script a hot property, they probably won't work very hard on your behalf. Sometimes a large agency will take you on as a **hip-pocket**, or temporary client, with no contractual obligation. As a hip-pocket client, you'll receive a short burst of attention and your script will probably be sent out to a few places. If the script doesn't generate heat, the agency will quickly write you off. You may have a better chance starting out with a small or mid-size agency. Though these agencies don't have the power that the big agencies do, they'll provide you with more support as you build your career.

Recently, lawyers and managers have played a more active role in scriptwriters' careers. Lawyers, like agents, may forward materials to studios and producers. Sometimes it's possible to get a good entertainment lawyer to represent your script without an agent. Be sure to research lawyers before you approach anyone. Recommendations are helpful so if you know anyone in the industry, ask questions before employing a lawyer. Some lawyers, like agents, will work on commission; some will charge an hourly rate. In some states (California among them), managers may not legally represent clients and forward client materials. Managers, who work on commission (sometimes greater than that of an agent or lawyer), may have useful connections and are more likely to give you personal attention. I'd caution you against managers unless you don't feel confident to strategize your own career. Everyone who becomes a player in your career takes an extra notch out of your paycheck. Of agents, lawyers, and managers, managers may be the most expendable. Of course, that's my opinion. You need to complete your own research before making any decisions affecting your career.

INDEPENDENT PRODUCTION COMPANIES

Since there's always a market for a good script, independent production companies are often willing to read a submission from a novice writer. Every year the Writer's Market publishes a writer's marketing book with an updated section devoted specifically to scriptwriting. The script section lists independent production companies that accept scripts, either through agencies or directly from writers. Each production company lists their specific needs and procedures for submission.

It helps to research independents and view the kinds of films they've made in the past. If you like the films and think your script might be suitable for their needs, you might want to call and get the name of a contact person. Secretaries or office assistants are often helpful, and if you conduct yourself in a friendly yet professional manner during the conversation, they may try to help you get your script to the right person.

On occasion, your call will be forwarded directly to someone within the development department. If that's the case, be sure you're prepared to pitch

the story over the phone. Your pitch may begin with a **logline**, a sentence that identifies the **genre** or type of your script and capsulizes the story. Read the summaries of movies in the *TV Guide* for models of loglines. A **pitch** is a quick-sell that describes the genre of your story, captures the listener's interest, highlights the unique properties of your story, and invites questions. The passion you feel for your story should be generated during your pitch. Just pretend you're telling your best friend about a great movie you saw. Practice your pitch before you call to make sure you feel confident about what you have to offer. Remember, you have something they may need.

If a producer requests that you send your script, they'll probably send you a **submission release form**. Studios or producers may not read your script unless they have a signed submission release form from you. A submission release form protects them from being sued if you have misrepresented yourself or your submission in any way or if your story closely resembles any other stories they might have in production. Sometimes a producer will ask that you sign a company release form. If that's the case, make sure the company forwards the form to you and that you sign it and enclose it with your script. Though submission release forms are standard practice, be sure to contact a lawyer if you're uneasy signing the form without legal advice.

If a producer requests your script, you might be able to use that as an entrée to an agency. Don't hesitate to contact an agency or an entertainment lawyer if a producer expresses genuine interest in your story. You should never negotiate an **option**, a contract giving the producer exclusive rights to your story for a fee for a limited time period, or a contract for purchase, without legal or agency assistance or both.

QUERY LETTERS

Unless an agent or producer solicits a script from you, you should send a query letter before submitting your script. This is appropriate professional etiquette that shouldn't be breached. If you send an unsolicited script, it will be returned to you unopened.

A **query letter** is a letter that introduces you and briefly describes your script to a potential agent or producer. It's extremely important that this letter be a thoughtful, inviting, and professional correspondence since it's the first (and perhaps only) contact you'll have with that agent or producer. First impressions go a long way. If you're claiming to be a writer, your letter needs to represent the best of your writing skills. This is essentially the first screening of you as a writer. If you can't write a powerful query letter, chances are no one will bother to look at your script.

There are some general guidelines to follow when sending a query letter. A good query letter usually doesn't exceed a page in length. Address the letter to a specific person—if you don't know who that is, find out. Be sure you properly spell the name of the person to whom the letter is addressed. It is appropriate to fax a query letter but only if you're prepared to send the script immediately should the agent or producer be interested. Never send a query letter for an unfinished script.

Make sure your letter has the following components:

- A succinct paragraph introducing you and setting a professional tone. If you have professional experience, you should cite it. If you've had unique life experiences, they might serve in lieu of professional experience. If you're a student, you don't need to mention it unless your films or scripts have garnered awards. Anything you write should help identify you as a competent professional. If you haven't any experience, you may want to briefly discuss why you're sending your script to that person. A sincere compliment about the producer's prior work is an appropriate opening as well.

- A brief synopsis of the script. Try not to exceed ten sentences. Be sure to include the story's genre. The objective is to capture the reader's interest without telling every detail.

- Don't be afraid to let your voice, your excitement, and your passion for your work resound throughout your letter. Just don't promise more than you can deliver.

- Make sure your letter is well written and that you've proofread it for grammatical errors.

- Express thanks and don't make demands upon the recipient.

If your query letter works, an agency or company representative will contact you requesting a copy of the script. Send the script, a standard release form, and an SASE (self-addressed, stamped envelope). Your script won't be returned without the inclusion of a postage-paid envelope.

Allow a month before you write a follow-up letter. Some writers even provide SASE postcards with choices for the recipients to check. If you provide choices, make sure they're either positive or neutral. Providing a negative choice is self-defeating. You might also keep a list or log documenting to whom the script was sent, when it was sent, and what the reply was.

If the agent or production company doesn't like your script, you probably won't hear anything from them. If you do receive a negative response, accept it gracefully. Move on and keep writing. Don't bank your success on one script. Build a body of work and don't quit your day job. As Janet Peoples, scriptwriter of *12 Monkeys*, advises: "It takes about ten scripts to really know what you're doing then usually a couple more to sell one, and

get one into production. You have to be committed to the process if you want to succeed."[8]

CONTESTS

Another viable means of marketing your scripts is through script contests. Though the competition may be tough, especially for the popular, national competitions, you shouldn't be intimidated. Contests may offer winners cash prizes, trips to conferences, free script consultation, publication of the results in a trade journal, a possible option, a stipend to work within the industry or with a professional mentor, the possibility of attaining an agent, or best of all, a script sale. For a list of recommended contests, consult the resource section.

THE DIGITAL REVOLUTION

Where once there were few paths to success along the journey, new paths and portals are opening to scriptwriters everywhere. Traditionally, filmmaking has been an elitist art controlled by a small circle of powerful people. With the advent of emerging technologies, filmmaking has become a more democratic art.

The Blair Witch Project is a perfect example of the new direction in which filmmakers are moving. According to the filmmakers the film was shot for around 33,000 dollars and grossed well over 200 million dollars worldwide. One of the unique aspects of *The Blair Witch Project* was the filmmakers' integration of computers and films. Instead of using the computer as a mere marketing tool, the filmmakers uniquely utilized the properties of the Internet to create a world that extended beyond the film. By building an extensive mythology on the Internet, they created an interest in the story long before anyone saw the film. The interactive site invited viewers to enter a world filled with mysterious findings, journal entries from one of the characters, artifacts, puzzles, hidden information, and endless dialogue concerning the veracity of the film.

No one could have predicted the success of *The Blair Witch Project*. The film's success is an indicator of the times. And there's no going back. Film critic Roger Ebert articulates the historical relevance of the digital revolution.

> Hollywood and the Internet are on a collision course. The Internet will survive, and so will those in Hollywood who understand it. But the day of the unwired mogul is over. The movie industry has the same relationship to the Internet today that it had to talkies in the 1920s: Plug in or quit . . . The next *Blair Witch* won't be promoted online—it will *be* online.[9]

What does this mean for you as a scriptwriter? It means that your options are as varied as your imagination. It means that for around 5,000 to 6,000 dollars you can buy a digital camera and computer complete with nonlinear editing software. With this system, you can shoot and edit your own film and download it onto the Internet, enter it in film festivals, or invent your own method of delivery. If you're not interested in directing your own film, you can get on the Internet and solicit a producer and director for your script. Or you can email your script to an agent or producer through a service. Or you can create a nonlinear, interactive story or game. Or you can create your own hybrid of the next generation of stories and storytellers. This may be the single most exciting time in history for a scriptwriter to explore storytelling.

In an excerpt from *Salon*, an online magazine, Senior Editor Scott Rosenberg discusses the role of interactive storytelling within the arts at large.

> Interactive artists—whether they produce CD-ROM movie-games or "serious hypertext," Web sites or live performances—want to use digital technology to share some of the power of creation with what used to be called their audience. The technology offers a kaleidoscope of new possibilities for participation and collaboration. In the past, artists who wanted to play around like this were limited to small groups in their immediate community; today, technology lets interactive artists reach a potentially mass-scale audience. And so they dream of what was once an impossibility: improvisation on a global scale; art with the depth of a classic, the immediacy of a video game and the reach of TV . . . But there's one problem they're still struggling to solve.
>
> How do you cede some measure of control or authority to the audience, reader, listener, "user"—yet still deliver a work that's expressive, moving, memorable, satisfying?[10]

Good question. And the answer isn't easy. Any new form creates new challenges—and new questions. Are there new paradigms for stories that will supplant or alter traditional storytelling? How do you protect your work once it's on the Internet? How do you make money as a writer on the Internet? These questions, as well as your own questions, will fuel necessary dialogue about the future of storytelling.

In her provocative work, *Hamlet on the Holodeck: The Future of Narrative in Cyberspace*, Janet Murray provides a context for understanding the evolution of stories.

> . . . we rely on works of fiction, in any medium, to help us understand the world and what it means to be human. Eventually all successful storytelling technologies become "transparent": we lose consciousness of the medium and see neither print nor film but only the power of the story

itself. If digital art reaches the same level of expressiveness as these older media, we will no longer concern ourselves with how we are receiving information. We will only think about what truth it has told us about our lives.[11]

JOURNEY'S END

Your truths are what inform your stories. And your stories are essential to the journey. Your best resources are your imagination and determination. If you persist, you will prevail. Your journey isn't complete until you've exhausted every possibility. Send your script to everyone who will look at it, shoot it yourself guerilla style, or brainstorm a new method of distribution.

If you haven't had any luck, never give up. Put your script aside and begin work on the next one. Write, believe in yourself, and pay close attention to the journey. The essence of the writing experience resides in the journey. And remember, the end of this journey is the beginning of the next.

Take a few minutes to reflect upon your journey. Where has it taken you and where do you hope to go from here? Envision yourself as the main character in a script of your writing life. How would you script the future? What changes will your character undergo on the journey? What obstacles will your character encounter? How will your character surmount these obstacles? Will your character be smiling at the end of the journey?

REFERENCES

1. Ethan and Joel Coen, *The Big Lebowski*, Working Title Films/Polygram Filmed Entertainment, 1998.
2. George Hickenlooper, ed., *Reel Conversations: Candid Interviews with Film's Foremost Directors and Critics*, Carol Publishing Group, New York, 1991, pp. 8–9.
3. Rita Mae Brown, *Starting from Scratch: A Different Kind of Writer's Manual*, Bantam Books, New York, 1988, p. 20.
4. Alia Yunis, "Writer With a View," *scr(i)pt*, Vol. 5, No. 6, p. 40.
5. Skip Press, *Writer's Guide to Hollywood Producers, Directors, and Screenwriter's Agents 1999–2000*, Prima Publishing, Rocklin, California, 1998, p. 11.
6. Nick Bantock, *The Forgetting Room*, Harper Collins Publishers, New York, 1997, p. 33.

7. Editors, *The Chicago Manual of Style*, Fourteenth edition, The University of Chicago Press, 1991, p. 133.
8. John Kim, "Production Companies: Getting Through the Door," *scr(i)pt*, Vol. 6, No. 2, p. 41.
9. Roger Ebert, "Sites Camera Action!" *Yahoo!* April 2000, p. 100.
10. Scott Rosenberg, "Clicking for Godot," *Salon*, October 2, 1997, http://www.salon.com/21st/feature/1997/10/02godot.html.
11. Janet H. Murray, *Hamlet on the Holodeck: The Future of Narrative in Cyberspace*, The MIT Press, Cambridge, 1999, p. 26.

PART III

Resources

BOOKS

On History

Framework: A History of Screenwriting in the American Film
The definitive history of the evolution of screenwriting in America. A valuable reference book for any scriptwriter. Tom Stempel, The Continuum Publishing Company, New York, 1988.

History of the American Cinema Series
The best, most comprehensive history of American cinema available. This multivolume series appeals to both the film scholar as well as the general reader and provides the scriptwriter with an overview of the evolution of the film industry. Charles Harpole, general editor. Charles Scribner's Sons/Macmillan Publishing Company, New York, 1990.

On Scriptwriting and the Writing Life

Adventures in the Screen Trade: A Personal View of Hollywood and Screen-Writing
Considered by many to be the "bible" of scriptwriting, Goldman's advice is timeless and his writing is always compelling. William Goldman, Warner Books, New York, 1989.

Alternative Scriptwriting: Writing Beyond the Rules
This second edition is even better than the first, helping the reader look beyond conventional scriptwriting. Included is a good chapter on structure and excellent case studies of films that defy formula. Ken Dancyger and Jeff Rush, Focal Press, Boston, 1995.

The Artist's Way: A Spiritual Path to Higher Creativity
Even if you don't consider yourself to be a spiritual person, this book will help you break through writing blocks and induce you to make writing a habit. Mark Bryan and Julia Cameron, JP Tarcher, New York, 1995.

Bird by Bird: Some Instructions on Writing and Life
A humorous book loaded with wisdom, it should definitely be a part of your library. Anne Lamott, Anchor/Doubleday, New York, 1995.

The Right to Write
Meditations on writing and all the nuisances that keep us from writing. Julia Cameron, J.P. Tarcher, New York, 1999.

Screenwriting from the Soul
Emulating Rilke's classic work, *Letters to a Young Poet*, Krevolin presents a practical as well as a philosophical treatise on scriptwriting. A good book to help you find balance between the craziness of the business and the

need to relish your writing life. Richard Krevolin, Renaissance Books, Los Angeles, 1998.

The Screenwriting Life: The Dream, the Job, and the Reality
A good primer for making the leap once you've completed your script. Interviews with writers and agents provide valuable real-world advice. Rich Whiteside, Berkley Boulevard Books, New York, 1998.

Wild Mind: Living the Writer's Life
A wealth of thought interspersed with ten-minute timed writings designed to tap your inner resources—a gem. Natalie Goldberg, Bantam Books, New York, 1990.

The Writer's Journey: Mythic Structure for Writers
This book is fast becoming a classic. Though the book draws from the psychology of Carl Jung and the mythic studies of Joseph Campbell, Vogler's voice rings through, bringing new understanding to the applications of traditional storytelling structures and archetypal characters. The second edition honestly addresses concerns and criticisms of the first edition and embraces alternate possibilities. Vogler has mounds of experience within the industry and remains open-minded. A powerful resource. Christopher Vogler, Michael Wiese Productions, Studio City, 1998.

Writing for Your Life: A Guide and Companion to the Inner Worlds
Helps you integrate your personal history, dreams, and journals to find your authentic voice. An essential book for anyone in search of the inner territory. Deena Metzger, Harper, San Francisco, 1992.

Writing from the Inner Self
Combines meditations and writing exercises to assist you on the journey to your inner self. Elaine Farris Hughes, Harper Perennial, New York, 1992.

The Writing Life
Full of wisdom and power, this book is invaluable for the serious writer. Written by a Pulitzer Prize winner. Annie Dillard, Harper Collins, New York, 1998.

Writing the Character-Centered Screenplay
Written in a scholarly style, this is my favorite book on character. Horton's unique voice and point of view shape a thorough and thoughtful exploration of character. Andrew Horton, University of California Press, Second Edition, 2000.

Zen and the Art of Screenwriting: Insights and Interviews
Considered a master teacher by many accomplished screenwriters, Froug offers sage advice and lively interviews with some of America's best screenwriters. William Froug, Silman-James Press, Beverly Hills, 1996.

Zen in the Art of Writing: Essays on Creativity Expanded
A celebration of life and the act of writing. Read it for the sheer pleasure. Ray Bradbury, Joshua Odell Editions, New York, 1994.

On the Digital Domain

Hamlet on the Holodeck: The Future of Narrative in Cyberspace
A fascinating book on the aesthetics of digital media as well as the future of nonlinear, interactive storytelling. Murray explores ideas of how to move interactive fiction from the formats of games into a mature art form. A must for anyone beginning to think about the future of storytelling. Janet H. Murray, The MIT Press, Cambridge, 1999.

On Marketing and Professional Opportunities

How to Enter Screenplay Contests & Win
Promises a little more than it delivers but still a worthwhile reference. Because new competitions may not be listed in the book, it's helpful to cross-reference with contests on the web as well. Erik Joseph, Lone Eagle Publishing Company, Los Angeles, 1997.

How To Sell Your Screenplay: The Real Rules of Film and Television
A thorough exploration of "how-to" market scripts for film, television, and alternative markets, written by an accomplished Hollywood writer. Carl Sautter, New Chapter Press, New York, 1988.

The Script Is Finished, Now What Do I Do? The Scriptwriter's Resource Book & Agent Guide
This second edition updates and embellishes an already strong book. The information is essential for serious scriptwriters. A list of agencies and some of their bankable clients as well as valuable interviews with agents are interspersed throughout the text. K Callan, Sweden Press, Studio City, 1998.

Writer's Guide to Hollywood Producers Directors and Screenwriter's Agents 1999–2000
A definitive reference book—a must. Sage professional advice as well as a wealth of information about agents, managers, producer, and director listings, screenwriting competitions—you name it. Skip Press, Prima Publishing, Rocklin, California, 1998.

On Legal Guidance for Scriptwriters

Clause by Clause: The Screenwriter's Legal Guide
Helpful legal advice for the screenwriter written by an entertainment lawyer. Includes sample contracts that are especially useful for

screenwriters who may want to produce their own work. Stephen F. Breimer, A Dell Trade Paperback, New York, 1995.

The Copyright Permission and Libel Handbook: A Step-By-Step Guide for Writers, Editors, and Publishers
This is a great reference book, especially if you want to determine if a work is in the public domain, wish to option a work that's copyrighted, or want to protect yourself from being sued. It's concisely written in language accessible to the layperson. Lloyd J. Jassin and Steven C. Schechter, John Wiley & Sons, 1998.

The Screenwriter's Legal Guide
This second edition, written by an attorney who's also a writer and producer, is a great primer on all legal aspects of the film and television industry. Pay special attention to the section on legal extras about which writers should be aware. Stephen F. Breimer, New York, Allworth Press, 1999.

The Writer Got Screwed (but didn't have to): A Guide to the Legal and Business Practices of Writing for the Entertainment Industry
Written in an animated style by a seasoned lawyer and teacher, this well-researched reference book is a valuable addition to your script library. The legal expertise is complemented by advice from working screenwriters as well. Brooke A. Wharton, Harper Perennial, New York, 1997.

BOOK AND SCRIPT SOURCES

Book City
Fax: (818) 848-5615
www.hollywoodbookcity.com

Collectors Book Store
1708 N. Vine Street, Box #2, Hollywood, CA 90028
www.members.aol.com/cobosto.cbs.html

Larry Edmunds Cinema and Theatre Bookshop, Inc.
6644 Hollywood Boulevard, Hollywood, CA 90028
Phone: (323) 463-3273

Samuel French Theatre and Film Bookshop
7623 W. Sunset Boulevard, Hollywood, CA 90046
Phone: (323) 876-0570

Fax: (323) 876-6822

www.samuelfrench.com

Script City

8033 Sunset Boulevard, Suite 1500, Hollywood, CA 90046

Phone: (818) 760-8292

www.scriptcity.net

CATALOG SOURCES

The Writers' Computer Store
You can order through the catalog or walk into one of their two locations. A must for the scriptwriter, features specialized section on film industry software, books, and tapes. 11317 Santa Monica Boulevard, Los Angeles, CA 90025-3118, phone: (310) 479-7774, fax: (310) 477-5314 or 3001 Bridgeway Avenue, Sausalito, CA 94966, phone: (415) 332-7005.
www.writerscomputer.com

The Write Stuff Catalog
Books, audiotapes, scripts, computer software, reference books, and accessories for writers of every type. A great selection with substantial resources for the scriptwriter. To order a catalog write: The Write Stuff Catalogue, 21115 Devonshire Street #182, Chatsworth, CA 91311, phone: (800) 989-8833 or (213) 622-9913, fax: (213) 622-9918.

COPYRIGHT AND REGISTRATION

To register your script with the copyright office, email, write, or call and request form PA and the instructions for registering your work. There is a fee for copyrighting your work. Register of Copyrights, Copyright Office, Library of Congress, Washington, DC 20559, phone: (800) 688-9889 or (202) 707-3000.
http://www.lcweb.loc.gov/copyright

To register your script with the Writers Guild, email, write or call for instructions on how to register. There is a fee. You may register your work with the Writers Guild West or East.
Writers Guild of America, West, 7000 W. Third Street, Los Angeles, CA 90048-4329, phone: (323) 951-4000.
www.wga.org

Writers Guild of America, East, 555 West 57th Street, Suite 1230, New York, NY 10019, phone: (212) 767-7834.
www.wgaeast.org

PERIODICALS

On Film and Television

Cineaste
Quarterly publication. Published from New York, it is heralded as the leading American magazine on the politics and art of cinema. Regular features cover articles related to the sociopolitical issues of third world and Eastern European filmmakers. Additional articles include film reviews and interviews with prominent filmmakers. P.O. Box 2242, New York, NY 10009-8917, phone: (212) 982-1241.
www.cineaste.com

Film Comment
Monthly publication by the Film Society of Lincoln Center. An aristocrat among film magazines, it makes a distinction between film reviews and film criticisms. Reports on festivals such as The New York Film Festival and the Cannes Film Festival. Its once-a-year index is divided into four parts: subject, author, film, and book review. An ideal resource for research. For more information about the Film Society or a subscription, contact: Film Comment, The Film Society of Lincoln Center, 70 Lincoln Plaza, 4th Floor, New York, NY 10023, phone: (800) 783-4903, fax: (212) 875-5636.
www.filmlinc.com

Film Quarterly
Quarterly publication by the University of California Press at Berkeley. Has a pool of respected contributing writers. Features include lengthy, thoughtful film reviews and interviews with leading international filmmakers. University of California Press at Berkeley, Berkeley, CA 94720, phone: (510) 642-4191, fax: (510) 642-9917.
www.-ucpress.berkeley.edu/journals/fq

MovieMaker: The Art and Business of Making Movies
Published six times a year, regular features include information on current film festivals and thoughtful articles on the art of film. Strong contributing writers share advice about both the process of making movies from script to screen as well as the business and legal aspects of filmmaking. 2265 Westwood Boulevard, PMB 479, Los Angeles, CA 90064, phone: (888) 625-3668, fax (310) 234-9293.
www.moviemaker.com

Premiere
   A monthly, mainstream magazine covering the popular American film and television industry. Regular features include interviews with popular film personalities, new film and video releases, future projects in development, along with industry gossip and trends. 2 Park Avenue, New York, NY 10016, (212) 481-6428. For subscription: Premiere Subscription Department, P.O. Box 55389, Boulder, CO 80323-5389, phone: (800) 289-2489.
   www.premieremag.com

Sight and Sound
   An international monthly magazine published by the British Film Institute. This very prestigious and widely read publication covers the international scene from various perspectives, offering articles on films in production, motion picture history, and the individual careers of classic film stars. The magazine also includes reviews of films, books, and current video releases. 1671 East 16th Street, Suite 176, Brooklyn, NY 11229.
   www.bfi.org.uk/s&s

On Independent Filmmaking/Screenwriting

Filmmaker: The Magazine of Independent Films
   The publication of the Independent Feature Project, an association created to support and nurture independent filmmakers. Membership benefits include reduced prices on software, equipment, and seminars. Articles include information on grants, the marketplace, film festivals, success stories of independent filmmakers, and new technologies. A must for the independent-minded filmmaker. 5455 Wilshire Boulevard, Suite 1500, Los Angeles, CA 90036-4201.
   www.filmMAG.net

Film Threat
   This publication is an alternative, anti-Hollywood, irreverent, mad look at filmmaking. It reminds you not to take yourself too seriously. 5042 Wilshire Boulevard, Suite 150, Los Angeles, CA 90036, phone: (626) 683-8245, fax: (626) 683-3170.
   www.filmthreat.com

The Independent Film & Video Monthly
   This magazine is a publication of The Foundation for Independent Video and Film. Membership benefits include reduced prices on software, equipment, and seminars. Articles feature successful independent filmmakers, information on emerging technologies, as well as information on grants and festivals. AIVF, 304 Hudson Street, 6 fl, New York, N.Y. 10013, phone: (212) 807-1400, fax: (212) 463-8519.
   independent@aivf.org

On Scriptwriting

Creative Screenwriting

This is the only scriptwriting publication designed for the academic community as well as the professional scriptwriter. The publication has recently been geared more for the practitioner. In-depth articles often focus on improving and expanding the craft of screenwriting. Guest scriptwriters share insiders' viewpoints and creative techniques. Every issue also includes trends, opportunities, information on New York and Los Angeles markets, educational seminars, and reviews of books and software for the serious scriptwriter. 6404 Hollywood Boulevard, Suite 415, Los Angeles, CA 90028, phone: (800) 727-6978, fax: (323) 957-1406.

www.creativescreenwriting.com

Hollywood Scriptwriter

Monthly newsletter. Has a solid reputation and originates from the heart of the industry. Features regularly include interviews with successful scriptwriters, articles on the writing and marketing of scripts, reviews of books and software, and updated information on contests, evaluation services, and production needs. P.O. Box 10277, Burbank, CA 91510, phone: (818) 845-5525, fax: (818) 709-7540.

http://hollywoodscriptwriter.com

scr(i)pt

Published bimonthly, this publication offers good interviews, updates on spec sales, pitches and competitions, reviews of books and software, and regular features on formatting and trends. 5638 Sweet Air Road, Baldwin, MD 21013-0007, phone: (410) 592-3466, fax: (410) 592-8062.

www.scriptmag.com

Written By (formerly *The Journal*)

Monthly journal except for a bimonthly December/January issue, it is the publication of the Writers Guild, available free to members. Since the Guild is actively involved in improving writers' lives and negotiating on behalf of writers, articles may focus on topics pertaining to wages, benefits, rights, power, and censorship. Regular features also include a TV market list, monthly calendar, and an FYI column providing writers with research references. Articles also address the writing life as well as interviews with practicing screenwriters. Writers Guild of America, West, 7000 West Third Street, Los Angeles, CA 90048, phone: (888) WRITNBY.

www.wga.org/WrittenBy

Trade Publications

Daily Variety

Daily, except weekends and holidays, this publication includes industry news that covers the "inside" reports on finances, ratings, box office returns, films and television in production, relevant news items, and classifieds. Available by subscription or online. Daily Variety, 5700 Wilshire Boulevard, Suite 120, Los Angeles, CA 90036, phone: (323) 857-6600 or (800) 323-4345.

www.variety.com

The Hollywood Reporter
Daily, except for weekends and holidays, this publication offers extensive reporting of industry news, including current works in production, ratings, box office, cable, video, DVD and digital news, production charts, and classifieds information. 5055 Wilshire Boulevard, 6th Floor, Los Angeles, CA 90036, phone: (323) 525-2150, fax: (323) 525-1082.

www.hollywoodreporter.com/

PRODUCTION DIRECTORIES

Hollywood Creative Directory
This publication, updated quarterly, offers extensive listings of mainstream and independent production companies on West and East Coasts. Single issue or yearly subscription. Also available online. Additionally, they have a library of other useful directories such as the Hollywood Agents & Managers Directory and the Hollywood Distributors Directory. 3000 W. Olympic Boulevard, Suite 2525, Santa Monica, CA 90404-5041, phone: (800) 815-0503, fax: (310) 315-4816.

www.hcdonline.com

Pacific Coast Studio Directory
In addition to updated information on production companies, this quarterly publication also includes information on agencies, guilds, and studios. Single issue or subscription available. P.O. Box V, Pine Mountain, CA 93222-0022, phone: (805) 242-2722, fax: (805) 242-2742.

www.studio-directory.com

SCRIPTWRITING COMPETITIONS

I've listed a few of those that have been around for awhile or that I feel confident are reliable. This is not intended to be an all-inclusive listing. The best way to research and enter competitions is on the web since there are always new competitions as well as discontinued contests. Most sites allow you to download entry forms as well. Never enter a competition without researching the organization first. If the sponsoring organization is not willing to share information about past winners or provide anything but a post office box with no phone, it may be a scam. The most comprehensive listing of competitions of which I'm aware is at www.moviebytes.com.

America's Best

An annual contest sponsored by The Writers Foundation that provides grants and awards for screenplays, television scripts, and comedy sketches/monologues. Cash prizes are awarded to winning screenplays; winning television scriptwriters may win a cash award, a studio visit, or a reading by producers; comedy writers may choose a cash prize or a grant to attend a comedy writing convention. Send SASE to: America's Best, c/o The Writers Foundation, Inc., 3936 South Semoran Blvd, Suite 368, Orlando, FL 32822, phone: (407) 894-9001, fax: (407) 894-5547.

Breckenridge Screenplay Competition

A newer festival so you may want to research this one. Attracts lots of stars if you're trying to cast your next low-budget film. Breckenridge Festival of Film, PO Box 718, Breckenridge, CO 80424, phone: (970) 453-6200, fax: (970) 453-2692.

www.brecknet.com/bff/home.html

Chesterfield Film Company Writer's Film Project

Prestigious festival with lots of heavy-hitters from the industry behind it. Winners receive a stipend to move to Los Angeles and work with a mentor from the industry. Very competitive. 1158 26th Street, Box 544, Santa Monica, CA 90403, phone: (213) 683-3977.

www.chesterfield-co.com

The Christopher Columbus Screenplay Discovery Awards

Unique since it runs a monthly and annual contest. Submit previously unproduced scripts. Prizes include an option of $10,000, professional development, advertising in trade journals, and access to industry professionals such as agents and producers. Writer must give option to purchase if selected. Deadline: December 1. Entry fee. Send SASE, application, and procedure to: The Christopher Columbus Screenplay Discovery Awards, #600, 433 North Camden Drive, Beverly Hills, CA 90210, fax: (310) 288-0257.

www.hollywoodnetwork.com

Cinestory Screenwriting Awards

Based in Chicago, this competition has grown in applicants as well as reputation. Lots of powerful industry support. A bit less orientated toward typical Hollywood scripts. For the true lover of good stories. 53 West Jackson, Suite 1224, Chicago, IL 60604, phone: (312) 322-9060.

www.cinestory.com

Heart of Film Screenplay Competition

A scriptwriter's dream. Winners attend a conference in Austin where they have the opportunity to interact with seasoned professionals. A great

experience. Austin Film Festival, 1604 Nueces, Austin, TX 78701, phone: (512) 478-4748, fax: (512) 478-6205.
www.austinfilmfestival.com

Maui Writers Conference Screenwriting Competition
Competitors attend a conference in Maui with great writers from various mediums. What more could you want? 2118 Wilshire Boulevard, Suite 726, Santa Monica, CA 90403-5784, phone: (808) 879-0061, fax: (808) 879-6233.
www.maui.net/~writers

Minority Screenwriters Development and Promotional Program
Send previously unproduced scripts. Founded to nourish and promote minority writers. Prize is $500 and exposure to industry. Send SASE for guidelines to: Minority Screenwriters Development and Promotional Program, Writers Workshop, P.O. Box 69799, Los Angeles, CA 90069-0799, phone: (213) 933-9232, fax: (213) 933-7642.

Nantucket Film Festival Screenplay Competition
Affiliated with their Annual Film Festival. A celebration of the scriptwriter. P.O. Box 688, Prince Street Station, New York, NY 10012, phone: (212) 642-6339, fax: (212) 473-0713.
www.nantucketfilmfestival.org

Don and Gee Nicholl Fellowships in Screenwriting
Send only unproduced screenplays. A maximum of five $25,000 fellowships are awarded each year. Deadline: May 1. Entry fee. Send SASE for application and procedure to: Don and Gee Nicholl Fellowships in Screenwriting, Academy of Motion Picture Arts and Sciences, 8949 Wilshire Boulevard, Beverly Hills, CA 90211-1972, phone: (310) 247-3059.
www.oscars.org/nicholl/index.html

Organization of Black Screenwriters Writers Competition
Dedicated to helping nurture minority writers. Great opportunity for unrecognized talents of minority writers. PO Box 70160, Los Angeles, CA 90070-0160, phone: (323) 882-4166.
www.obswriter.com

Scriptapalooza
A new upstart in the competition neighborhood. You might want to do some research on this one. 775 Sunset Boulevard, Suite #200, Hollywood, CA 90046, phone: (323) 654-5809, fax: (323) 656-7260.
www.scriptapalooza.com

Slamdance Screenplay Competition
Affiliated with the Slamdance Film Festival, founded as an alternative to Sundance. Because Sundance has been criticized for becoming

increasingly commercial, Slamdance presents an alternative for independent filmmakers and writers. 6381 Hollywood Boulevard, No. 520, Los Angeles, CA 90028, phone: (323) 466-1786.
www.slamdance.com

The Sundance Institute
Submissions for feature film scripts are accepted twice a year. The selection committee will only select a synopsis for the first round of applicants. Those selected participate, with nine other writers, in a month-long workshop in June or a four-day workshop in January. Send SASE for information about philosophy of the institution, description of program, deadlines and entry fee. The Sundance Institute, 225 Santa Monica Boulevard, 8th Floor, Santa Monica, CA 90401, phone: (310) 394-4662, fax: (310) 394-8353.
www.sundance.org

Walt Disney Studios Fellowship Program
Resembles the old studio days. Winners work on the lot with mentors and receive a stipend. Terrific opportunity. Fellowship Program Administrator, Walt Disney Pictures & Television, 500 South Buena Vista Street, Burbank, CA 91521-0880, phone: (818) 560-6894.

SCREENWRITING SOFTWARE

Screenwriting software has come a long way. You should research for yourself to see what features you most desire. Features you might look for are: templates for film, television, and playwriting, ability to email a whole script document, writing for nonlinear stories, ability to create A and B pages, and ability for the program to read dialogue aloud assigning different voices to each character. Almost all the programs have a sample you can download to see what features are available.

Final Draft, Inc.
16000 Ventura Boulevard Suite #800, Encino, CA 91436, phone: (800) 231-4055 or (818) 995-8995, fax: (818) 995-4422.
www.finaldraft.com/html/index.html

Movie Magic Screenwriter
Screenplay Systems, Inc., 150 East Olive Ave., Suite #203, Burbank, CA 91502-1849, phone: (818) 843-6557, fax: (818) 843-8364.
www.screenplay.com

Script Thing
Script Perfection Enterprises, 4901 Morena Boulevard, Suite #105, San Diego, CA 92117-3424, phone: (800) 450-9450, fax: (619) 270-2523.
www.scriptperfection.com

Scriptware
Cinovation, Inc., 1750 30th Street, Suite 360, Boulder, CO 80301-1005, phone: (800) 788-7090.
http://scriptware.com

Story Vision
Solely a multimedia ware. Available through The Writer's Computer Store.
Sanfrancisco@writerscomputer.com

WEBSITES

This is by no means a definitive list. It's also one that may need to be updated frequently since websites often morph into new sites or become defunct. To my knowledge, all the listed sites are free.

The Future of Digital Storytelling—Food for Thought

Digital Film Festival
An annual digital storytelling festival. You can attend in person or online. Great links to explore digital storytelling.
http://www.dstory.com/

Digital Storytelling: Is It Art?
A provocative he said/she said between Sven Birkerts (author of *The Gutenberg Elegies*) and Janet Murray (author of *Hamlet on the Holodeck*). Join in the debate or link to other sites as you explore questions related to the future of storytelling.
http://hotwired.lycos.com/synapse/braintennis/97/31/indexOa.html

Online Digiplex

AtomFilms
Primarily designed for distribution of shorts and animation. Drawback—slow download time but otherwise a terrific site.
www.AtomFilms.com

D. Film
Home of the Digital Film Festival, this sites plays shorts from the festival, clips from the features, interviews with the directors, and information for exchange of equipment, talent, etc. Some of the most innovative filmmaking on the web.
www.dfilm.com

Ifilm
This site is dedicated to serious independent short films, many of which are already festival award winners. Only drawback is that most films require RealPlayer. This site is expanding so watch for new resources.
www.ifilm.com

MediaTrip
You can download quality shorts, trailers, and feature films from this site. Also features music videos, interviews with filmmakers, and weekly Internet TV shows. A great digiplex—the only drawback is having to provide personal info to have access.
www.MediaTrip.com

The New Venue
A sophisticated site that showcases the best in experimental, digital films.
www.newvenue.com

Online Zine

Cinezine
A free, weekly online publication. Offers the latest industry news, box office grosses, etc.
Email CineZine@aol.com with "Subscribe" in the subject line.

Opportunities

Done Deal
. Free site that offers in-depth interviews with established agents, writers, and managers. A chance to meet fellow writers and mentors online. Opportunity to sell your books or scripts in the Done Deal bookstore.
www.Scriptsales.com

Hollywood Literary Sales
Sponsored by Black and Blue Entertainment and the Steve Tisch Company, you may submit a logline for your script. If they like it, they will request a one-page synopsis. If they like the synopsis, they'll read your script. Also a great site to research. If you need information on medicine, forensic science, the military, etc., you may email your questions and a consultant will reply.
www.hollywoodliterarysales.com

Hollywood Script
You can have your query letters evaluated before you circulate them at this site.
www.hollywoodscript.com

Kingman Films International

Founder and CEO Arthur C. Chang accepts pitches and query letters via email. Be prepared to send a synopsis. In-house readers look at the synopsis and review material. Writers must agree to keep the material propriety for a 30-day period, though writers may withdraw in writing should they receive another offer during that period. Select scripts will be developed and produced.

www.kingman-films.com

Scriptnet

You can post your screenplay title, genre, logline, synopsis, and contact information for consideration by producers who hold a password to the site. The site is free for three months with no obligation to continue after that.

www.zest.net/ScriptNet

Zoetrope: All Story

Links to Francis Ford Coppola's production company complete with a discussion page. If you provide good coverage for four other writers' scripts, you have the opportunity to submit your script for coverage. Scripts with the highest praise will be forwarded to the company for consideration.

www.Zoetrope.com

Organizations

Writers Guild of America

The bible of screenwriting sites. Fabulous research links. Excerpts of *Written By* articles. In-depth software reviews. Agents and agencies listing and more.

www.wga.org

Research and Resource Sites

Ain't It Cool News

Developed by Harry Knowles, it's become a hot site frequented by studio heads who phone him directly. Knowles is the man in the know.

www.aint-it-cool-news.com

Celluloid Jungle

A literary reference site that offers you rhymes, cliches, quotations, a thesaurus, encyclopedias, and libraries. Great links to other reference sites.

www.celluloid-jungle.com

Cinemedia Search Engine
Part of the American Film Institute online. Billed as "The Internet's largest film and media directory." Search for information about almost everything in the media, including film festivals, schools, and magazines.
www.ptd15.afionline.org/CineMedia/cmframe.html/

Coming Attractions
One of the best sites to see what's in development.
www.corona.bc.ca./films/mainFramed.html/

Indiewire
The site for the serious filmaker. A must!
www.indiewire.com

Internet Movie Database
The definitive site for the cinephile offering the most in-depth film research tool on the Internet. Search for titles, actors, directors, writers, posters, box office receipts, studio news, etc.
www.imdb.com

Law Girl
An entertainment lawyer specializing in trademark, music and new media. She'll answer questions regarding entertainment/intellectual property via her Legal Board.
www.lawgirl.com

The Mad Screenwriter's Page
A good place to search for literary references. Also has a great crime writing link.
http://fade.to/madscreenwriter

Moviebytes
Extremely comprehensive information about screenwriting contests, festivals, competitions, and workshops. Invaluable.
www.moviebytes.com

Research-It!
Writer's resource. Extensive references, including dictionary, translator, thesaurus, people search, quote search, and maps.
www.iTools.com/research-it/research-it.html/

Screaming in the Celluloid Jungle
Hollywood–centered. Industry news and in-depth information about script sales.
www.celluloidjungle.com

Screenwright (R) WORDS
Another writing resource. Contains a thesaurus, dictionary, translator, and database of cliches, anagrams, and acronyms.
www.apc.net/ia/scrword.htm/

Screenwriters & Playwrights Home Page
Extensive links to writing and screenwriting resources. Information about everything from script registration to analyzing scripts.
www.teleport.com/~cdeemer/scrwriter.html

Screenwriters Utopia
You can receive advice on how to write great query letters at this site.
www.screenwritersutopia.com

Writers Write
An internet writing journal with a screenwriting section. Great writing and screenwriting links.
www.writerswrite.com

Scripts Online

Drew's Script-O-Rama
A vast archive of film and television scripts. You can even compare drafts of scripts. Downloadable, too. Not all are in proper script format. Gathered from a variety of sources—some may be questionable.
www.script-o-rama.com

Free Movie Scripts
TV and film scripts online.
www.freemoviescripts.com

ScreenTalk's Movie Script Gallery
A long list of screenplays from which to choose.
www.screentalk.org/gallery.html

Scriptshop
An online catalog of film and television scripts. Order your script online and have it delivered to your home.
www.scriptshop.com

Simply Scripts
Hundreds of current, classic, and soon-to-be-released scripts.
http://simplyscripts.home.att.net

Printed in Great Britain
by Amazon.co.uk, Ltd.,
Marston Gate.